VANISHED

PLANES THAT DISAPPEAR

CHRIS MCLEOD

VANISHED

Planes that disappear into thin air and the mysteries surrounding those that crash

A Boeing 777 carrying 239 passengers vanishes on a flight from Kuala Lumpur to Beijing.

Ten months of extensive searching on land and in the ocean find no trace of it. No wreckage, no bodies. No word of it at all. Was it hijacked? Did it crash?

More than 100 planes and the people on them have disappeared without trace in the history of aviation.

Flight 370 of Malaysia Airlines, that disappeared in March 2014, created one of the biggest mysteries. But another major shock was to come for Malaysia Airlines. Yet another Boeing 777, on a flight from Amsterdam to Kuala Lumpur, was blasted out of the skies five months later, taking the lives of all 298 people on board. Who shot it down? Why?

The passage of time and a more scientific approach to investigations was likely to provide some answers to these mysteries. But it was going to take time, maybe even years.

There have been no answers to many mysteries over more than a century. Where did Amelia Earhart disappear to? Was Amy Johnson shot down by friendly fire? What was the fate of Smithy and Ulm? What really happened to Air France 447 and TWA 800? Why have so many planes been lost in the Bermuda Triangle?

Investigations have sometimes produced answers but they weren't always believed.

MALAYSIAN DISASTERS
699 PEOPLE LOST ON 3 FLIGHTS

Wreckage from Malaysia Airlines flight MH17 lies in a field on July 22, 2014 in Grabovo, Ukraine

Three passenger jets associated with Malaysian-based airlines disappeared from the skies in 2014, claiming 699 lives and shocking the world

Malaysia Airlines was hit hard – two passenger jets lost in just 5 months: one simply vanished from the skies in March; the other was blown out of the sky in July. Gone were 537 people that were aboard them.

Then in December a passenger jet from budget airline Indonesia AirAsia, an affiliate of Malaysian-based AirAsia, disappeared on a flight from Surabaya in Indonesia to Singapore, with 162 people on board.

The biggest mystery was what happened to MH Flight 370 after it left Kuala Lumpur for Beijing on 8 March. The best information available suggested the plane crashed into the Indian Ocean somewhere west of Australia after deviating dramatically – and inexplicably - off its planned course.

Months of searching above, on and under the ocean had failed to find any trace of the plane.

The shooting down of MH flight 17 on a flight from Amsterdam to Kuala Lumpur on 17 July sparked international outrage and sharply increased international tensions between Russia and the West, with Russia at the centre of accusations about its support for the separatists in Ukraine believed responsible for shooting down the plane.

As usual, there were conspiracy theories, none of which seemed likely at first examination. Nevertheless the World seemed convinced that the two MH flight disasters involved some form of deliberate human action or intervention.

While claims and counter claims were still being exchanged over that incident and searches continuing for MH 370, the world was stunned on 28 December to learn that AirAsia flight QZ8501, on its way to Singapore, had lost contact with air traffic controllers. Though no distress signals were detected it was widely believed the plane had crashed into the Java Sea.

Was this another MH 370? Probably not – the circumstances of the disappearance of the Airbus were more likely closer to those surrounding an Air France crash in 2009 whether severe weather was a contributing factor. And this time, debris and bodies were found within 3 days of the plane's disappearance.

GOOD NIGHT MALAYSIAN THREE SEVEN ZERO

AIR TRAFFIC CONTROL: Malaysian Three Seven Zero contact Ho Chi Minh 120 decimal 9, good night.

MH370: Good night Malaysian Three Seven Zero.

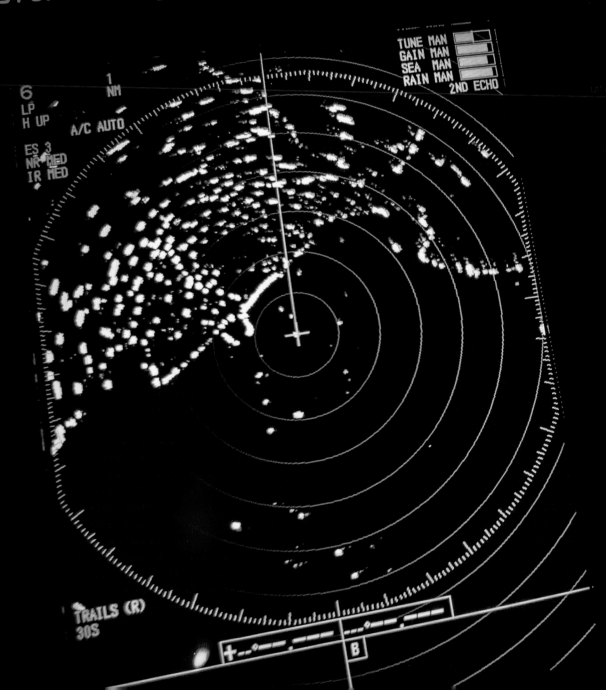

With that exchange Malaysia Airlines Flight MH370 seemingly passed into oblivion on the night of 8 March 2014.

Facts were few and far between in the aftermath.

THE ACCEPTED FACTS:

- Flight MH 370 was carrying 12 Malaysian crew members and 227 passengers from 14 countries.

- The flight departed from Kuala Lumpur International Airport on 8 March 2014 at 00:41 local time and was scheduled to land at Beijing Capital International Airport at 06:30 local time.

- It climbed to its assigned cruise altitude of 35,000 feet and was travelling at 471 knots (872 km/h) true airspeed (the speed of the aircraft relative to the air mass in which it is flying) when it ceased all communications and the transponder signal was lost

- There was no further direct contact with the plane from that point, but its Satellite Data Unit continued to communicate through an Inmarsat satellite over the Indian Ocean via seven electronic "handshakes".

- The aircraft's last known position on 8 March at 01:21 local time was at the navigational waypoint IGARI in the Gulf of Thailand, at which the aircraft turned west, heading towards a waypoint called VAMPI in the Strait of Malacca.

- On 8 March 2014 at 07:24, Malaysia Airlines (MAS) reported the flight missing.

No distress signal was received and there were no reports of bad weather or technical problems.

The plane's planned route should have taken it northeast, over Cambodia and Vietnam, and the initial search focused on the South China Sea, south of Vietnam's Ca Mau Peninsula.

The crew of MH370 had been expected to contact air traffic control in Ho Chi Minh City as the plane passed into Vietnamese airspace. There was no contact.

No distress signal was received and there were no reports of bad weather or technical problems.

In May, a preliminary report on the investigation by the Malaysian Government said air-traffic controllers and Malaysia Airlines weren't able to determine what was happening but military radar saw the plane appear to go back on its course.

The aircraft was classed as "friendly" by the military operator and no further action was taken.

After Vietnam air traffic controllers failed to contact Flight 370 on various frequencies, Malaysian controllers began querying authorities in Hong Kong, Beijing and Singapore about possible contact. The plane was assumed then to have crashed.

Singapore sent a C130 Hercules to the search area to look for debris. A submarine rescue vessel with a submersible sonar tracking device was also sent to help search in the Gulf of Thailand. Nothing was found.

Evidence from military radar, revealed later, and the satellite "handshakes" suggested the plane had suddenly changed from its northerly course to head west across the Malay Peninsula, turned north again before it apparently turned south off the western tip of Sumatra and continued south in a straight line over the Indian Ocean.

More than 7.5 hours after take-off the plane was expected to have run out of fuel.

So the search, by then involving dozens of ships and planes, switched to the sea west of Malaysia.

A week after the plane's disappearance, the search was expanded dramatically to nearly 3 million square miles, from Kazakhstan in the north to vast areas of the remote southern Indian Ocean.

CONFUSION

It was established that radar tracked the aircraft as it turned sharply off its scheduled northeast flight path, passing over the Gulf of Thailand and flying west across the Straits of Malacca. It then passed out of radar range near the northern tip of the Indonesian island of Sumatra.

Malaysia's ambassador to China told Chinese families in Beijing as early as 12 March, four days after the flight went missing, that the last words with the plane had been "all right, good night". But that was considered unusual language and raised speculation about what might have happened in the cockpit.

Then on 1 April, 2 weeks later, Malaysia's Department of Civil Aviation issued this statement: "We would like to confirm that the last conversation in the transcript between the air traffic controller and the cockpit is at 0119 (Malaysian Time) and is 'Good night Malaysian 370.'" Still later, Malaysia confirmed the words were spoken by the pilot.

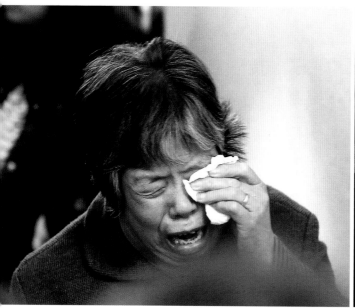

By then Malaysian authorities faced heavy criticism for their handling of the plane's disappearance, particularly from families of the Chinese passengers on board who had accused Malaysia of mismanaging the search and withholding information.

The conflicting statements about the last contact marred what appeared to be a genuine effort by Malaysian authorities, particularly Acting Transport Minister Hishammuddin Hussein who gave daily and sometimes more regular briefings to the media and families, to keep everyone up to date.

What first captivated the world's attention was the possibility that the plane was hijacked, either by a passenger or one of the crew.

What first captivated the world's attention was the possibility that the plane was hijacked, either by a passenger or one of the crew.

The revelation that two passengers had used stolen passports to board the plane was thought to be a clue, then discounted.

Several times questions were raised about whether the pilot, Captain Zaharie Ahmad Shah, or the co-pilot, Fariq Ab Hamid, had taken the plane off its flight path deliberately.

Interest was heightened with the revelation that Captain Shah had built a flight simulator in his home. But there was no evidence he used it for improper purposes, such as

plotting to crash the plane or land it somewhere other than Beijing. There was no obvious motive for such an action and his family was adamant he would not have done such a thing.

As much as relatives of those aboard didn't want to confront the logical conclusion, it was hard to argue that the plane had not crashed somewhere, most likely into the ocean.

A crash on land was discounted because someone would have seen it or found debris. Even a "normal" landing should not have gone unnoticed and Malaysian officials said China, India, Myanmar, Laos, Kyrgyzstan and Khazakhstan all confirmed their radars had not picked up any sign of the missing plane.

On March 15, Malaysian authorities said they believed "deliberate action" caused the plane to veer off course and someone had shut down its tracking systems. Suspicion again enveloped the cockpit crew, but still there was no real evidence to implicate the pilot or co-pilot. The plane's flight recorders would probably hold the answers, if they could be found.

Eventually, Malaysian Prime Minister Najib Razak announced that analysis of satellite information determined that the aircraft's flight ended somewhere in the Indian Ocean and all on board would have perished.

Over ensuing weeks and months the search area was redefined each time new analysis was provided. An Australian team co-ordinated the search focussed on the Southern Indian Ocean. But success was elusive.

MORE CLUES BUT NO ANSWERS

At the end of June a report issued by Australian investigators revealed that the Boeing 777 had suffered a brief power outage early in the flight.

According to the report, the plane's satellite data unit made an unexpected "log-on" request to a satellite less than 90 minutes into its flight.

The request, known as a handshake, was likely to have been the result of an interruption to electrical power on board the plane and would be considered uncommon during a flight.

The revelation again prompted speculation: had the power been shut down deliberately by someone on board?

The Australian Transport Safety Board also said it was confident the Boeing 777 was set to autopilot several hours before its demise in unmapped waters. It was also likely passengers had suffocated before the plane fell.

Adding to the mystery were the conspiracy theories that grew out of the vacuum created by the lack of tangible evidence.

Even aliens were considered suspects. According to the Daily Mail newspaper, a survey in the US found one in 10 people believed "space aliens or beings from another dimension were involved" in the disappearance of MH370.

The world's media outlets dwelt on every statement from the Malaysian officials, putting their own interpretations on what was said or not said, without much attention paid to cultural differences that could affect interpretation.

Frustrating for many was the inability to sheet blame home to anyone in particular. There was no credible claim of responsibility by a terrorist organisation. There was no firm evidence to implicate anyone in particular.

Relatives became more frustrated. Many refused to accept that their loved ones were gone.

A protest at the Malaysian embassy in Beijing called on the Malaysian government to reveal the "truth" about Flight 370's whereabouts.

Other groups started raising money for a reward to encourage whistleblowers to come forward and tell all.

But without the plane, speculation was all the world had.

And predictions were for an extremely long wait for only a slight hope of resolution.

THE QUESTIONS

- Why did the plane make a sharp turn and fly thousands of kilometres off its scheduled course?

- How did the plane's automatic communications systems, particularly the transponder, become inoperative?

- If the plane was hijacked, what was the purpose? Why had no one claimed responsibility?

- If there was a catastrophic mechanical failure, why hadn't this been recorded by air traffic controllers, the airline, or even the plane's makers if they were receiving "live" information from the plane?

- If the plane crashed or was destroyed, why was no debris found?

- Could the plane have been shot down? Deliberately, or accidentally?

- Was there a brief power outage and if so did that mean someone had tampered with the aircraft's systems?

- With a significant number of sophisticated spy stations and military installations around the world, why didn't someone realise there was a large plane that was where it shouldn't be and raise the alarm? In particular, if the plane flew towards the southern Indian Ocean, why didn't the Australian over-the-horizon radar Jindalee Operational Radar Network (JORN) see MH370?

- After three months, none of these questions had been answered to the satisfaction of relatives of the people on board.

WHERE IN THE WORLD?

...nding out what happened to MH370 was a two-pronged investigation: Malaysian authorities were trying to find the cause of the presumed crash and Australian authorities were leading the search in the Indian Ocean for the plane.

One of the first reports was that the plane had landed in Nanning, China. According to the airline company (MAS) this wasted an hour of search time. It had not landed there and as best as anyone could establish it had not landed anywhere else.

The likely crash site was at first considered to be the South China Sea. It was over the sea that the last conversation between the plane and air traffic controllers took place. Reports of debris were checked but eventually discounted. Possible locations in the Gulf of Thailand, the Strait of Malacca along Malaysia's west coast and the Andaman Sea also were checked and discounted when no debris from the plane could be identified and oil slicks that were spotted could not be linked to the plane.

When it was revealed that Thai military radar had detected a plane, accepted as MH370, making a sharp turn left towards the Strait of Malacca, speculation was it had a problem and the pilot was trying to get to a safe landing somewhere, perhaps an island. But with no landing reported, the conclusion was that the plane crashed into the ocean.

On 17 March, Australia agreed to lead an aerial search of the Indian Ocean from Sumatra south, with planes operating out of Pearce Air Force base near Perth, Western Australia.

Search planes included a US Navy P-8 Poseidon and Australian, New Zealand, South Korean and Japanese maritime surveillance P-3 Orions.

Two Chinese Ilyushin Il-76s and two C-130 Hercules planes from Malaysia also took part in operations from Pearce.

Ships from Australia, China, Malaysia and a submarine from the United Kingdom conducted water searches.

On March 20 debris was sighted in the search area, heightening speculation that searchers were homing in on the crash site. Australia, the United Kingdom, the United States, China, Japan, New Zealand and South Korea assigned military and civilian ships and planes to the area.

French satellites also spotted debris.

All the sightings proved to be false leads, only serving to point to the amount of rubbish in the ocean.

But on 24 March, the Malaysian prime minister announced that after more analysis of satellite data it was beyond doubt that the plane had gone down in this part of the ocean.

Independent analyses by the British Air Accidents Investigation Branch (AAIB) and British satellite company Inmarsat had firmed up a route over the Indian Ocean west of Western Australia as the most likely one taken by MH370. Search efforts were to be concentrated in that area by a Joint Agency Coordination Centre (JACC) under the leadership of Retired Air Chief Marshal Angus Houston of Australia.

On 29 January 2015 the Malaysian Government declared the loss of MH370 and all on board as an accident, to enable the compensation process to proceed.

Australian Government
Australian Maritime Safety Authority

·Kuala Lumpur

·Jakarta

Australian Search and Rescue Region Boundary

I n d i a n   O c e a n

·Perth

·Canberra

Planned search areas
(24 March 2014)

S o u t h e r n   O c e a n

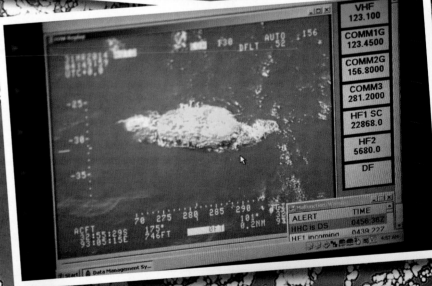

VHF
123.100

COMM1G
123.4500

COMM2G
156.8000

COMM3
281.2000

HF1 SC
22868.0

HF2
5680.0

DF

ALERT | TIME
HHC is DS | 0456.38Z
HF1 incoming | 0439.22Z

Start | Data Management Sy...

Main Pic: A piece of unknown debris floats just under the water in this image taken onboard a Royal New Zealand P3 Orion while it searches for missing Malaysia Airlines flight MH370, over the Indian Ocean on March 31, 2014

Inset top: A Satellite image made available by the AMSA (Australian Maritime Safety Authority) shows a map of the planned search area for missing Malaysian Airlines Flight MH370

Inset bottom: A picture taken off a computer monitor shows the unknown debris

I SAW IT .... MAYBE

Two separate people reported sightings near Malaysia which they said could have been Flight MH370 on fire

A passenger on another plane reported seeing a large plane down in the Bay of Bengal. A mineral search organisation said it may have detected a plane wreck. But searchers stuck to the likely flight paths that were determined from Inmarsat satellite data analysis.

THE OIL RIG WORKER

The first reported sighting came to light several days after the disappearance. A New Zealand man working on an oil rig off the south-east coast of Vung Tau, Vietnam, claimed he saw a plane "come down" in flames.

Mike McKay detailed his coordinates and passport number in an email to authorities in which he says he tried to contact officials in Malaysia and Vietnam "several days ago" but did not know if the message had been received.

"I believe I saw the Malaysian Airlines plane come down. The timing is right," Mr McKay said in the email.

"I observed (the plane?) burning at high altitude. While I observed the burning (plane) it appeared to be in ONE piece."

He sent officials the coordinates of the oil rig he was working on, the surface sea current and wind direction, and estimated the plane to be about 30-45 miles away.

"From when I first saw the burning (plane) until the flames went out (still at high altitude) was 10-15 seconds. There was no lateral movement, so it was either coming toward our location, stationary (falling) or going away from our location," he wrote.

Vietnam said it sent a plane to investigate but found nothing.

If the report was accurate, it placed missing flight MH370 near where it was originally believed to have disappeared off the radar.

In a twist to this event, New Zealand daily newspaper the Sunday Star Times reported 2 months later Mr McKay had been dismissed from his job. He had been working on the Songa Mercur oil rig.

His email to his employers was leaked to the media. It contained details which identified the rig operator, Idemitsu, and the contractor Songa Offshore, details which led to the 2 companies having their communications blocked due to a flood of inquiries.

Vietnamese officials interviewed Mr McKay and were prepared to act on his information before search efforts shifted to the Andaman Sea 2 days after his interview.

Mr McKay had also made a statement for Interpol upon his return to New Zealand.

A member of the Indonesian Air Force at Medan city military base inspects the Indonesian military search operation for the missing Malaysian Airlines flight MH370

THE SAILOR

Sailor Katherine Tee filed a report in May with the Australian led Joint Agency Coordination Centre (JACC) saying she may have seen MH370 on fire as it passed in their air near her yacht.

Ms Tee said that in March, she was sailing from Cochin, India, to Phuket, Thailand, when a figure of a plane on fire illuminating the night sky caught her attention. The plane had black smoke in spiral shape trailing behind it.

"All I can confirm is that I have since learnt that we were in the right place at the right time, so it seems possible, but I chose to sweep it under the carpet and now I feel really bad. Maybe I should have had a little more confidence in myself. I am sorry I didn't take action sooner," Ms Tee told the Phuket Gazette in June.

She began reviewing her yacht's Global Positioning System (GPS) log after hearing a report that a survey ship was going back to port because of technical difficulties. Checking her log with data maps on routes across the Indian Ocean she realised that she may have seen the plane.

A map created by a member of Cruisers Forum by using Google Earth showed the missing plane would have passed where Tee's yacht was at the time if reports about it tracking to the southern Indian Ocean were accurate.

"This is what convinced me ... to file a report with the full track data for our voyage to the relevant authorities," Ms Tee said.

I saw something that looked like a plane on fire. That's what I thought it was. Then, I thought I must be mad...

"I saw something that looked like a plane on fire. That's what I thought it was. Then, I thought I must be mad ... It caught my attention because I had never seen a plane with orange lights before, so I wondered what they were. I could see the outline of the plane; it looked longer than planes usually do. There was what appeared to be black smoke streaming from behind it," Ms Tee recalled.

She said there were 2 other planes passing above the apparently burning plane, flying to the opposite direction. The other planes had the usual navigation lights.

"I remember thinking that if it was a plane on fire that I was seeing the other aircraft would report it. And then, I wondered again why it had such bright orange lights. They reminded me of sodium lights. I thought it could be some anomaly or just a meteor." she said.

Ms Tee said she regretted not reporting what she saw as soon as she came back from her sailing trip on the night of 10 March. She said she was afraid that the information would be dismissed together with other reported sightings at the time.

THE SAUDI AIRLINES PASSENGER

A Malaysian woman, Mrs Latife Dalelah, claimed to have seen a plane in the water near the Andaman Islands while on a flight crossing the Indian Ocean on the day MH370 disappeared.

She said she saw an aircraft-shaped object while on a Saudi Airlines flight to Kuala Lumpur about 2.30pm local time on 8 March. She said she told a flight attendant what she'd seen, but was told to get some sleep.

Mrs Dalelah insisted she saw a silver object in the shape of an aircraft on the water as she was flying from Jeddah to Kuala Lumpur. It was about an hour after her aircraft had flown past the southern Indian city of Chennai.

When her plane landed at Kuala Lumpur about 4pm that Saturday she told her children what she had seen. "That is when they told me that MH370 had gone missing," she told the New Straits Times.

She filed a report with police at the urging of her son-in-law, a police officer.

Former commercial pilots were sceptical, saying a sighting was highly improbable from commercial flight 35,000-feet up.

THUMP

The Marine Science department at Curtin University, Perth, Australia, said it was investigating a mysterious low-frequency underwater noise detected off the southern tip of India about the time the Malaysia Airlines plane made its last satellite transmission and disappeared.

The noise, originating almost 5,000 km north-west of Australia, was thought to have travelled across the Indian Ocean and been picked up by the university's receivers that usually monitor whales.

Dr Alec Duncan, a marine scientist at Curtin University, said: "It's not even really a thump sort of a sound — it's more of a dull oomph. If you ask me what's the probability this is related to the flight, without the satellite data its 25 or 30 per cent, but that's certainly worth taking a very close look at."

According to the New York Times on 3 June, the sound also was picked up by another monitor, 350 km south of Perth, operated by the Comprehensive Nuclear Test Ban Treaty Organisation in Vienna.

An acoustics expert at the test ban organisation headquarters told the Times the sound was consistent with an ocean impact or with a sealed, air-filled container sinking until it crumpled under water pressure.

GEORESONANCE

The GeoResonance company which had been conducting a private search since 10 March told an Australian television network it had detected objects that were possibly from a plane wreck in the Bay of Bengal near the Andaman Sea.

According to GeoResonance, elements it detected on the ocean floor were consistent with the elements of an aircraft.

GeoResonance, a company based in Adelaide, Australia, claims to operate nuclear magnetic resonance technology capable of detecting subsurface deposits of minerals using satellites. The technology has potential use in oil exploration and groundwater exploration and in the identification of potential resources for mining.

In April 2014 GeoResonance claimed it had identified a metallic deposit in the Bay of Bengal which could have been the remains of Malaysia Airlines Flight 370.

GeoResonance said it identified the location by comparing satellite imaging data collected on 5 March and 10 March in the Bay of Bengal. This, it said, showed a significant difference in the amount of copper, titanium, and other substances consistent with the construction of the plane.

On June 30, the GeoResonance web site carried the following statement: *GeoResonance stands by its claim that we have located what appears to be the wreck of an aircraft 190 kms South of the Bangladesh coastline in 1,000 to 1,100 metres of water. We have never claimed this to be MH370, however it is a lead that must be thoroughly followed through. It has been confirmed that the precise location supplied by GeoResonance to all authorities involved in the search for MH370 has not been searched.*

THE LEADS

Fresh examination of 8 satellite "pings" sent by the aircraft between 1.11am and 8.11am local time on Saturday 8 March (when it vanished from radar screens) had put the plane over the Indian Ocean heading south, in a corridor a couple of hundred miles wide. A revised search area was established.

Malaysian Prime Minister Najib Razak, said: "Based on their new analysis, Inmarsat and the AAIB have concluded that MH370 flew along the southern corridor, and that its last position was in the middle of the Indian Ocean, west of Perth."

Chris McLaughlin, senior vice-president for external affairs at Inmarsat, told Sky News: "Unfortunately this is a 1990s satellite over the Indian Ocean that is not GPS-equipped. All we believe we can do is to say that we believe it is in this general location, but we cannot give you the final few feet and inches where it landed. It's not that sort of system."

Special search equipment from the United States including the unmanned submarine Bluefin-21 was called in. Detection devices towed by search ships were also used.

The search was urgent. Without finding the plane itself or any debris, the best hope was to find the plane's flight recorders before their batteries expired.

On 28 March the main search area was moved 1,100km (684 miles) to the north-east and closer to Australia. This followed further analysis of the speed of the plane and its maximum range.

On 5-8 April, Australian and Chinese vessels, with underwater listening equipment, detected ultrasonic signals, which it was thought could be from the plane's "black box" flight recorders. The pings appeared to be a promising lead, and were used to define the area of a sea-floor search by the Bluefin-21 submersible robot.

By 29 May the search had found nothing and the area where the signals were heard was ruled out as the final resting place of the plane. Efforts would now focus on reviewing data, surveying the sea floor and bringing in more specialist equipment.

Australian naval vessel Ocean Shield had been sent to investigate the area identified by Inmarsat as the most likely ending of Flight MH370. But before reaching the likely site, it began to detect a signal in a different area, believed to be from the plane's flight recorders.

On 6 April Ocean Shield towing a locator device detected a number of pings said to be consistent with those from an aircraft.

On 14 April the Bluefin-21 Autonomous Underwater Vehicle was brought into the search in the area where the pings were heard.

Two months were spent searching 850 sq km of sea bed north-west of Perth, but the source of the "pings" was not found and a submersible robot found no evidence of the plane. Estimates put the amount spent on the search to that time at $US100 million.

It was speculated that the pings had actually come from search ships or the equipment they were towing.

By this time a dozen countries had taken part in the search for MH370.

BACK TO THE 7TH ARC

After almost 3 months of fruitless searching, the focus was switched again, reverting to the original area identified by Inmarsat: the "seventh arc", one of a series of possible routes or arcs the plane could have taken as identified by analysis of the final satellite "handshake" with flight MH370.

There was no new data, just more analysis of information from Inmarsat and other sources.

The most likely flight path was determined by using the hourly pings and assuming a speed and heading consistent with the plane being flown by autopilot.

The 60,000 sq km search area, about 1,800km from the West Australian coast, had been searched from the air previously but the new effort was to head into the water, along the ocean floor and 5 km (3 miles) deep in parts.

The new search phase had 2 elements: mapping the sea floor and a comprehensive below-water search.

On 10 June, the Australian Transport Safety Bureau (ATSB) announced a $AU 90 million, 3-month contract with the Dutch deep sea survey company Fugro Survey Pty Ltd to map a wide part of the seafloor in the "hot spot" area.

The project was to begin in August and was expected to take up to 12 months, depending on weather conditions.

Malaysia Airlines (MAS) commercial chief Hugh Dunleavy conceded the search could take decades.

Retired Air Chief Marshal Houston said in June it could take more than two years to find the plane.

He said the search was an even harder task than that for an Air France jet that was eventually located just 6.5 nautical miles from its last known location.

I think you've just got to be a little bit patient here, just hark back to Air France. The aircraft was found 6.5 nautical miles from its last known position and it took 2 years to find it," he said.

THE ROLE OF INMARSAT

The key information about the whereabouts of MH370 came from Inmarsat, a British satellite communications company.

Inmarsat provides telephone and data services worldwide via portable or mobile terminals which communicate with ground stations through 11 geostationary telecommunications satellites. Clients include governments, aid agencies, media outlets and businesses that need to communicate in remote regions or where there is no reliable terrestrial network.

Inmarsat told the Malaysian Government on 13 March that routine automatic communications between its satellite and MH370 could be used to determine several possible flight paths. A "northern corridor" and "southern corridor" were identified as the most likely paths taken by MH370.

On 24 March, the UK Air Accidents Investigation Branch provided the Malaysian Government with Inmarsat's most recent findings which identified the southern corridor as the most likely path.

After vanishing from radar, MH370 continued to respond to hourly pings from Satellite INMARSAT 3F-1, the responses ending around the time the plane would have run out of fuel. The probable flight path was calculated from those pings.

AAIB's report explained that if the ground station did not hear from an aircraft for an hour it would transmit a log-on/log-off message – a "ping" – and the aircraft would automatically return a short message indicating that it was still logged on, a process described as a "handshake".

The ground station log recorded 6 complete handshakes after ACARS, the aircraft's operational communications system, stopped sending messages.

- Inmarsat was founded in 1979 as the International Maritime Satellite Organisation, a not-for-profit international organisation, set up for the International Maritime Organization (IMO), a UN body, to establish a satellite communications network for the maritime industry. The name was changed to International Mobile Satellite Organization when it began to provide services to aircraft and portable users but the acronym Inmarsat was kept. When the organisation became a private company in 1999, the business was split into two parts: the commercial company, Inmarsat, and a smaller unit, the IMSO regulatory body.

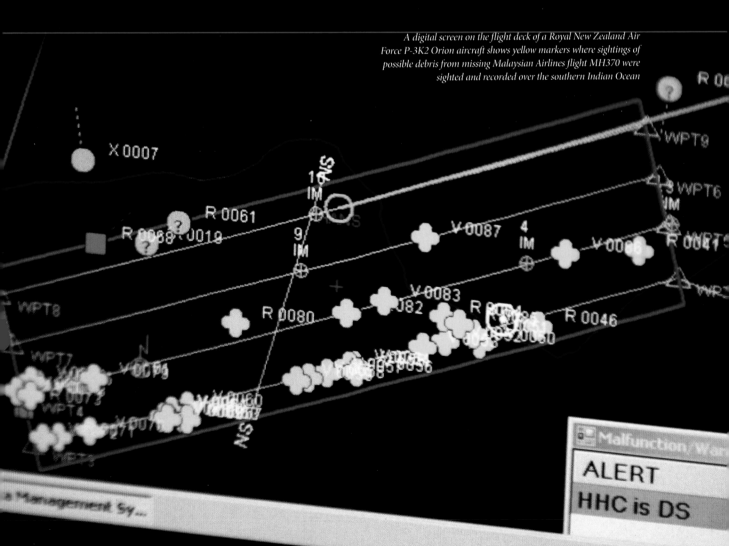

A digital screen on the flight deck of a Royal New Zealand Air Force P-3K2 Orion aircraft shows yellow markers where sightings of possible debris from missing Malaysian Airlines flight MH370 were sighted and recorded over the southern Indian Ocean

THEORIES AND CONSPIRACIES

PLANE WAS SHOT DOWN DURING MILITARY OPERATIONS

A quick-release book claimed MH370 may have been accidentally shot down by US-Thai strike fighters as part of a training drill that went horribly wrong and the search for survivors covered up.

If it was an accidental shooting, though hard to believe, no one would want the embarrassment or liability that would follow by confessing.

DEPRESSURISATION

If there was an air leak, or the plane flew too high or someone intentionally interfered with the plane's operations in some way, pressure might have been reduced, causing people, including crew, to fall asleep and eventually die due to lack of oxygen.

CIA KNOWS

Former Malaysian Prime Minister Mahathir Mohamad was reported as having accused the CIA of knowing the whereabouts of flight MH370. He said someone was hiding something because if the plane's GPS system failed then Boeing or the US government agency would know why. He also claimed the plane could be controlled remotely.

US MILITARY BASE CONSPIRACY

A current airline executive and a former executive of another airline both cast doubt on the southern Indian Ocean theories.

Sir Tim Clark, head of Emirates Airlines, said he disagreed with the hypothesis that the Beijing-bound jet crashed into the Indian Ocean after running out of fuel.

As far as Sir Tim is concerned, it is virtually impossible for an aircraft of that size to go missing off the face of the earth in this modern day and age. Someone is withholding information, he says.

Marc Dugain, former head of the French Proteus Airlines, says he believes there was a cover-up in the disappearance of MH370. He was convinced the Malaysian Airlines passenger plane crashed near the Indian Ocean island of Diego Garcia.

His view was that the plane was probably hijacked (by remote control) and maybe even shot down by the US either by mistake or out of fear that it was to be used in a terrorist attack on the US base at Diego Garcia. His basis: witness accounts from people on the islands of the Maldives who described seeing a plane that appeared to match the livery of MH370.

The United States flatly denied claims the plane landed at its military base on the remote island of Diego Garcia in the Indian Ocean which had been an early claim.

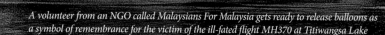

A volunteer from an NGO called Malaysians For Malaysia gets ready to release balloons as a symbol of remembrance for the victim of the ill-fated flight MH370 at Titiwangsa Lake

AFGHAN HIJACKING

A Russian newspaper claimed MH370 was hijacked and flown to Afghanistan, where the crew and passengers were being held captive. A report said the plane was in Afghanistan not far from Kandahar near the border with Pakistan.

MH370 HID BEHIND ANOTHER PLANE

Early in the search it was suggested that the plane may have been hijacked and hidden from detection in the shadow of another plane, possibly Singapore Airlines flight 68, as it passed through Indian and Afghani airspace.

STOLEN FOR USE IN A TERRORIST ATTACK

An extraordinary theory was that the plane was stolen by terrorists to commit a 9/11 style atrocity. It landed safely, was hidden or camouflaged, and would be refuelled and fitted with a new transponder and later used to attack a city.

A LIFE INSURANCE SCAM

Malaysian police were asked if it was possible the disappearance of the plane was part of an elaborate insurance scam. They said authorities were exploring every single avenue, no matter how remote.

FIRE

One of the most widely held theories was that fire killed all on board but burned out before damaging the exterior of the plane. This would explain why the aircraft, on auto-pilot, would fly such a long distance off course, said proponents.

Alternatively, MH370 may have been heading to the Malaysian resort island of Langkawi to land after the transponders were knocked out by a fire.

A SECRET WEAPON AT WORK

Conspiracy theory and scientific web site Natural News offered this: "If we never find the debris, it means some entirely new, mysterious and powerful force is at work on our planet, which can pluck airplanes out of the sky without leaving behind even a shred of evidence. If there does exist a weapon with such capabilities, whoever controls it already has the ability to dominate all of Earth's nations with a fearsome military weapon of unimaginable power."

PILOT SUICIDE

One explanation for the sudden disappearance, according to some, could be pilot suicide.

But there was no evidence to suggest either captain Zaharie Ahmad Shah or co-pilot Fariq Abdul Hamid had such intentions. A Malaysia Airlines spokesman said: "We have no reason to believe that there was anything, any actions, internally by the crew that caused the disappearance of this aircraft."

CRACKS IN THE AIRCRAFT

Six months before the plane went down, the US Federal Aviation Administration warned airlines of a problem with cracks in Boeing 777s that could lead to mid-air break up and catastrophic drop in pressure.

The FAA warned that failure to rectify this possibility would leave the aircraft vulnerable to a rapid decompression and loss of structural integrity. Boeing said that the FAA alert did not apply to the missing jet because it did not have the same set-up as the rest of the Boeing 777s.

TERRORISTS CRASHED IT INTO THE SEA

No terrorist groups claimed responsibility for hijacking the flight, but to some it was a credible explanation.

The two passengers who boarded the plane with stolen passports sparked speculation about terrorism, even though their actions were explained.

Pray for
MH370

#PrayForMH370

HOPE

Screen

#PRAY FOR MH370

Our thoughts and prayers go out to the passengers, crew members and families of all on board MH370
- gan

#PrayForMH370

MH370

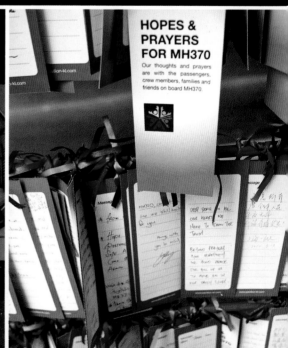

HOPES & PRAYERS FOR MH370

Our thoughts and prayers are with the passengers, crew members, families and friends on board MH370.

FLIGHT 370

THE PLANE

Flight 370 was operated with a Boeing 777-2H6ER, serial number 28420, registration 9M-MRO. According to records it was the 404th Boeing 777 built and first flew on 14 May 2002. It was delivered new to Malaysia Airlines on 31 May 2002. It was powered by 2 Rolls-Royce Trent 892 engines and configured to carry 282 passengers.

The plane had accumulated 53,460 operating hours and 7,525 take-off and landing cycles. It had not previously been involved in any major incidents, though a wing tip was broken in a minor incident while taxiing at Shanghai Pudong International Airport in August 2012. Its last maintenance A-check was on 23 February 2014. A-checks are performed after around 500 to 800 flight hours or 200 to 400 cycles and takes from 20 to 50 man-hours.

The Boeing 777, introduced in 1994, is generally regarded as having a safety record among the best of all commercial planes.

Since the first 777 commercial flight in June 1995, there had been 3 other accidents involving hull-loss: British Airways Flight 38 in 2008; a cockpit fire in a parked Egyptair 777-200 at Cairo International Airport in 2011; and Asiana Airlines Flight 214 in 2013 in which 3 people died.

THE CREW

The pilot was Captain Zaharie Ahmad Shah, a Malaysian aged 53. He had a total 18,365 flying hours and joined Malaysia Airlines in 1981. First officer was Fariq Abdul Hamid, a Malaysian aged 27. He had a 2,763 flying hours and joined Malaysia Airlines in 2007.

Suspicion of Capt Zaharie emerged within a week of MH370's disappearance when detectives raided his home in Kuala Lumpur and took away his home-made flight simulator.

Friends and relatives denied Capt Zaharie had any motive for hijacking his own plane and described him as a warm and helpful man committed to social work.

Then on 23 June it was reported the pilot was again under suspicion. Investigators allegedly had found that the pilot had plotted and deleted a flight path to an unnamed remote island far in the southern Indian Ocean on his home-made plane simulator.

Despite a lack of any hard evidence or motive, suspicion of Capt Zaharie's involvement grew as investigators eliminated other potential suspects and causes of the plane's disappearance.

The media got excited again about the captain. "Recovered Simulator Files Show Possible Devious Intent By MH370 Pilot" trumpeted one web site. Other outlets, led by The Sunday Times, reported Captain Zaharie had become the prime suspect in the plane's disappearance.

These reports were debunked immediately by Malaysian officials: Acting Transport Minister Hishammuddin Tun Hussein described publication by the Sunday Times as irresponsible.

Inspector-General of Police Secretariat assistant head (corporate communications) ACP Asmawati Ahmad also described the reports as irresponsible and baseless.

She said: "We replied (to an inquiry by the newspaper) that investigation was still ongoing, not conclusive and encompassed all aspects of investigation. We did not make

a statement that Captain Zaharie was the main suspect in the incident."

Back to square one. Detectives and investigators, including experts from Britain's Air Incident Branch, had after almost 3 months found no evidence of a technical fault or malfunction.

Inquiries into the backgrounds of the flight's passengers and crew had also failed to yield any evidence of, or motive for, anyone hijacking the plane or sabotaging it.

Adding fuel to speculation was a report that Investigators had concluded MH370 was probably not seriously damaged in the air and remained in controlled flight for hours after contact was lost, until it ran out of fuel over the southern Indian Ocean.

It was likely the plane was operating on autopilot. But who had engaged it?

CARGO

Items on Malaysia Airlines' cargo manifest issued on 1 May included 3 to 4 tonnes/tons of mangosteens, 221 kg of lithium-ion batteries and 2,232 kg of radio accessories and chargers.

The batteries obviously represented a source of fire, but according to the airline they had been packed according to specifications.

Many believe the full cargo manifest was being withheld.

THE PASSENGERS

The discovery that 2 men on the Malaysia Airlines flight had stolen passports raised speculation of a possible terrorist link, but it is was later established that they were asylum seekers heading for Europe via China. The passports had been stolen in Thailand.

The passengers included a group of famous Chinese artists and the director of Nanjing Painting and Calligraphy Academy, 20 employees of a Texas semiconductor

firm, a Hollywood stuntman and a pair of Malaysian honeymooners.

Ju Kun was a stuntman in Hollywood, doubling for martial arts actor Jet Li in *Fearless* (2006) and *The Expendables* (2010). Ju was on his way to visit his children in Beijing before starting work on Marco Polo, a new Netflix and Weinstein Company series being shot in Malaysia.

The employees of Texas-based Freescale Semiconductor, which produces microchips for a variety of applications and customers including the military, were Malaysia and China nationals.

On 18 March the Chinese government said it had checked all of the Chinese citizens on the aircraft and ruled out the possibility that any were potential hijackers.

According to Malaysia Airlines, the nationalities of the passengers on the flight manifest were: 153 Chinese; 38 Malaysian; 7 Indonesian; 6 Australian; 5 Indian; 4 French, 3 American, 2 each from New Zealand, Ukraine and Canada; one each from Russia, Taiwan, Netherlands; and the 2 men, one confirmed as Iranian, travelling under stolen Italian and Austrian passports.

SUSPECTS

With investigators not finding suspects among the crew and passengers, suspicion turned elsewhere.

On May 4, newspapers reported that a group of 11 people, with alleged links to al-Qaida, were arrested on suspicion of involvement in the jet's disappearance.

The suspects, aged between 22 and 55, were arrested in the Malaysian capital Kuala Lumpur and the state of Kedah.

9M-MLP

They were alleged to be members of a new terror group and included students, odd-job workers, a young widow and business professionals.

No direct link to the plane's disappearance was established.

On 9 March, Chinese news media received an open letter claimed to be from the leader of the Chinese Martyrs Brigade, a previously unknown group.

The letter claimed that the loss of flight MH370 was in retaliation for the Chinese government's response to the knife attacks at Kunming railway station on 1 March 2014 and part of the wider separatist campaign against Chinese control over Xinjiang province's Uyghur regions. The letter also listed unspecified grievances against the Malaysian government.

The claim was dismissed as fraudulent, based on its lack of detail regarding the fate of MH370 and the fact that the name "Chinese Martyrs Brigade" appeared inconsistent with Uyghur separatist groups which describe themselves as "East Turkestan" and "Islamic" rather than "Chinese".

LAW SUITS

MAS and the Government said they would provide $US 50,000 as initial aid to families of those lost on MH370. A decision on final amounts would only be made when the aircraft was found, they said.

It was reported that passengers' families could claim up to about $US 175,000 under International Civil Aviation Organisation rules, regardless of fault, in a plane crash.

Malaysia Airlines braced itself for the inevitable round of legal action.

According to Malaysian transport law specialist Mr Jeremy Joseph, it was an airline's responsibility under international law to prove it was not to blame for an accident.

"On the surface, (Malaysia Airlines) is responsible," he said. The "burden of proof" rested on the national carrier to clear its name.

Legal action had to be filed within 2 years of an accident.

Within 3 weeks of the disappearance of MH370 law firms in the US started lodging actions to get information. Other firms encouraged relatives of those on board to contact them.

BOOKS AND MOVIES

Books and movies were in production before the search for MH370 was 100 days old.

First out was English author Nigel Cawthorne, who canvassed in his book Flight MH370: The Mystery the possibility that MH370 was shot down by mistake during a US-Thai military exercise.

Two New Zealanders, Ewan Wilson, a commercial pilot, and Waikato Times journalist Geoff Taylor, claimed in their book that the MH370 tragedy was no accident.

Good Night Malaysian 370: the truth behind the loss of Flight 370, according to the authors, presented a detailed analysis of the flight, the incredible route it took, and who it was believed in charge of the aircraft as it plunged into the Indian Ocean.

Wilson, a former CEO of two airlines, and Taylor say they investigated every piece of evidence and travelled to Malaysia to interview authorities and family members of MH370's pilot, Zaharie Ahmad Shah.

American aviation author Christine Negroni, who wrote Deadly Departure about TWA Flight 800, also began working on a book called Crashed, to be published by Penguin.

A movie at first said to be about missing Flight MH370 was promoted at the Cannes Film Festival in 2014.

Rupesh Paul Productions promoted The Vanishing Act, with a poster promising to tell "the untold story" of the missing plane, but associate director Sritama Dutta said the only similarities between the thriller and the real-life disaster is that a plane was missing.

REPERCUSSIONS

At the end of June, Malaysian Prime Minister Najib Razak replaced acting Transport Minister Hishammuddin Hussein, who was in charge during the first 3 months of the search for missing flight MH370.

Liow Tiong Lai, a former health minister and president of the Malaysian Chinese Association (MCA), became Transport Minister. Hishammuddin Hussein retained the post of Defence Minister and continued to play a part in the investigation.

Lloyd's of London insurers faced big hits on its 2014 profits with hundreds of millions wiped out by the two Malaysia Airlines disasters. Industry estimates for MH370 payouts were $US 100 million.

MAS announced it would install pioneering technology from British satellite firm Inmarsat that would enable a signal to be sent out if a plane deviated from its flight path. MAS was also reported to be considering a restructure of its business, including a new brand name for the airline.

A proposal with options to allow better aircraft tracking was to be drafted by the International Air Transport Association. IATA, which represents 240 airlines, was working with the United Nations International Civil Aviation Organisation.

Boeing was reportedly seeking patents for advanced flight recording devices.

Inmarsat announced a free service expansion to include global tracking and monitoring for any aircraft with Inmarsat hardware installed, estimated to be 80-89% of all planes.

OUR DEEPEST CONDOLENCES

We are all deeply saddened by the news of MH370.
Our sincerest condolences go out to the loved ones of the
239 passengers, friends and colleagues. Words alone
cannot express our enormous sorrow and pain. They have
left us too soon, but they will never be forgotten.
They will forever remain in our thoughts and prayers.

From the Board of Directors,
Management and Staff of

*A full-page advertisement placed by Malaysia Airlines
appearing in the national daily paper The Australian*

Members of the public, MAS staff, and politicians pray during a special prayer as the search for missing Malaysian airline MH370

WHAT GOES UP MUST

It is hard to believe in the 21st Century that a large passenger plane carrying 250 people could just disappear without trace or even be shot down. Yet Malaysia Airlines was on the receiving end of two catastrophes in 2014

While unusual, cases of a plane disappearing have occurred relatively regularly. Cases of airliners being shot down are much rarer.

According to The Aviation Safety Network, 88 aircraft have been declared "missing" since 1948. Another dozen remained missing for several weeks and even years before they were found and answers unravelled. Add those lost without trace in the wars and on peaceful service before 1948 and the number of missing planes is in the many hundreds.

Of those lost in peacetime without trace, 62 were believed to have crashed into the sea.

The words of Isaac Newton are relevant:

"What goes up must come down."

"A man may imagine things that are false, but he can only understand things that are true."

Some explanations were relatively easily established by investigators – mechanical failure, pilot error, extreme weather, for example. Even when an airliner has been shot down, the effect is clear but the cause may not be.

Today, planes are highly sophisticated. So is search equipment.

COME DOWN

Logic dictates that every plane that has disappeared came down somewhere. But where evidence of its crash or landing is not immediately evident, there will be speculation about its fate, some of it wild, some of it with just a whiff of authenticity.

Pinning down the exact cause can take years, and sometimes there may never be a clear-cut answer.

The busiest time for plane searches was from 1960-1979. In 1964, 87 crashes claimed 1597 lives on flights carrying a total of just 141 million passengers.

Absent any witnesses to a crash, fire and debris are the first signs of an aerial disaster. Modern planes equipped with tracking technology also give off electronic signals that allow their position to be determined. Without those clues, investigators have very little to go on.

Despite the grim record, travel by plane remains one of the safest means of transport.

AirlineRatings figures for 2014 shows there were 21 fatal accidents claiming 986 lives, higher than the 10-year average, but a record considered satisfactory for 27 million flights carrying 3.3 billion passengers. About 6 million people around the world board a plane each day.

AirlineRatings acknowledged Australian airline Qantas as one of the world's safest and most experienced airlines over its 94-year history and a world leader in real-time satellite monitoring of engines across its fleet. Others in the AirlineRatings top 10 safest of the 449 airlines it reviews were Air New Zealand, Cathay Pacific, British Airways, Emirates, Etihad, EVA Air, Finnair, Lufthansa and Singapore Airlines.

<u>Author's note:</u> For the purposes of readability, figures used are those in the form given by investigators and official reports, whether they are metric or imperial. Information on disappearances has been gleaned from media reports, official investigations and findings as well as various websites and publications dedicated to particular incidents.

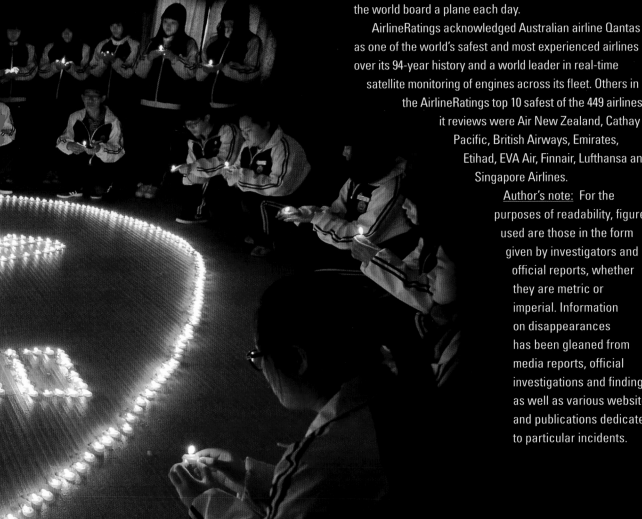

Indian sand artist Sudersan Pattnaik gives final touches on a sand sculpture
with a message of prayers for the missing Malaysian Airlines flight MH370

malaysia

do Happen

BLACK BOXES

The flight recorders aboard MH370 held the main hope of finding out what happened to the plane

Dubbed "black boxes", they aren't even black and are not usually referred to as "black boxes" within the industry. They are coloured "international orange", a set of three colours used in aerospace and engineering to distinguish objects from their surroundings.

The electronic flight data recorders keep detailed track of flight information; data such as altitude, position and speed as well as all pilot conversations. Many civil airliners have multiple devices for these tasks so information can be gathered more easily in the event of a failure. In most instances, they are used to help determine what may have been the likely cause of an accident.

The flight recorders however don't offer much help in cases of sudden catastrophe, such as missile attack.

Digital recorders have enough storage for 25 hours of flight data but only two hours of Cockpit Voice Recording. The CVRs track the crew's interactions with each other and air traffic control, but also background noises.

They aren't even black and are not usually referred to as "black boxes" within the industry. They are coloured "international orange", a set of three colours used in aerospace and engineering to distinguish objects from their surroundings.

Flight recorders originated in Australia. Dr David Warren's father died in a Bass Strait plane crash in 1934 when David was 9 years old. In the early 1950s, Dr Warren had an idea for a unit that could record flight data and cockpit conversations to help investigators piece together the events that led to an accident. He wrote a memo for the Aeronautical Research Centre in Melbourne called A Device for Assisting Investigation into Aircraft Accidents and in 1956 produced a prototype flight recorder called the "ARL Flight Memory Unit".

The units eventually were manufactured in the UK and US. Australia was the first country to make the technology compulsory.

The recorders are fitted with an underwater locator beacon that starts emitting a pulse if its sensor touches water. They work to a depth of 4 kilometres (2.5 miles) and can "ping" once a second for 30 days before the battery runs out.

AREN'T BLACK

Honeywell

FLIGHT
RECORDER
O NOT OPEN

SOLID STATE MEMORY COCKPIT VOICE RECORDER

Honeywell

SUSPICION AND THEORIES

A plane goes down or disappears. Mechanical failure could not be established. Some of the people aboard were famous. So what really happened? That's fertile ground for conspiracy theories

FLIGHT 777-A, DOUGLAS DC-3, 1943

On 1 June 1943, 8 German Junkers Ju 88S warplanes fired on British Overseas Airways Corporation (BOAC) flight 777-A, operated by Dutch airline KLM, which crashed into the Bay of Biscay killing all 17 people on board.

A notable passenger was English actor Leslie Howard, hardly a target for a German air strike unless later theories that Howard was actually a British spy had some credence.

The passengers on the Douglas DC-3 included Howard, who had returned from Hollywood to help the British war effort, and his tax adviser, Alfred Chenhalls.

The presence of Chenhalls gave rise to another theory. He smoked cigars and looked somewhat like Winston Churchill. Did the Germans believe that Churchill was on board Flight 777-A?

Other aircraft flying that route went unchallenged by the Luftwaffe which had a strong presence over the Bay of Biscay.

During World War II, British and German civilian planes operated out of the same facilities at Portela airport at Lisbon, Portugal, and the incoming and outgoing traffic would have been studied by Allied and Axis spies. Planes on the Lisbon–Whitchurch route flown by Flight 777-A often carried agents and escaped prisoners of war to Britain.

The Dutch pilot's last message: "I am being followed by strange aircraft. Putting on best speed ... we are being attacked. Cannon shells and tracers are going through the fuselage. Wave-hopping and doing my best."

A former German pilot said in a book published after the War that BOAC Flight 777-A was not intentionally targeted but was accidentally shot down when mistaken for an Allied military aircraft.

The day after the BOAC flight was shot down, a Short Sunderland flying boat from the Royal Australian Air Force's 461 Squadron searching the area was also attacked but the crew managed to shoot down 3 attackers before crash-landing at Penzanze, Cornwall in England.

GLENN MILLER, NORSEMAN C-64, 1944

Renowned band-leader Glenn Miller was aboard an RAF Norseman C-64 on the way from England to Paris on 15 December 1944. But the plane never arrived, believed to have crashed into the English Channel in fog.

Miller was a major in the Army Air Force, the military aviation service of the US during and immediately after World War II, and was going to join the rest of his band to play for troops in the recently liberated French capital.

Few people knew Miller was missing at the time: the plane disappeared the same day the Germans launched their last major offensive against the Allies in what would be known as the Battle of the Bulge.

What happened to the single-engine Norseman 10 days before Christmas has never been determined and no trace of the plane, or Miller, was found.

Recent speculation has been that the plane was brought down either by a German fighter or friendly fire, specifically ordnance being dropped by a fleet of British Lancaster bombers on their way back from a cancelled bombing mission. Bombers couldn't land with unexploded ordnance on board and had to jettison their bomb loads—preferably over the ocean.

MYSTERY ON THE MON, 1957

There are theories to the contrary, but the Air National Guard Mitchell B-25 bomber that disappeared on 31 January 1956 most likely still sits somewhere at the bottom of the Monongahela River outside Pittsburgh.

The B-25 trainer was running low on fuel on a flight from Nellis Air Force Base in Nevada to Olmstead Air Force Base in Harrisburg and the crew was trying to make it to Greater Pittsburgh Airport. But the fuel ran out and the plane ditched in the river.

Six of the crew survived the crash itself but 2 perished in the icy water. For 2 weeks after the crash searchers found no trace of the plane.

For the people of Pittsburgh, until the plane is recovered the many theories and rumours could still be true. Giving weight to some theories is that 1956 was at the height of the Cold War and Pittsburgh was surrounded by several missile bases.

According to gossip, the bomber was carrying a secret cargo of anything from a nuclear weapon, nerve gas, Mafia money to even Howard Hughes or Las Vegas showgirls.

There were accounts at the time that hundreds of soldiers appeared along the river after the crash and locked down the site. There was even a story of a seventh person being plucked from the water.

Other reports were that barges were brought in, the plane raised and taken away on railcars to local steel mills and melted down.

There were also reports of witnesses being threatened if they spoke of what they saw.

A B-25 Recovery Group was formed and over the years has pieced together the witness accounts, discounting most of the speculation.

The group remained confident of pinpointing the resting place of the B-25, most likely under 10 to 15 feet of silt in 32 feet of water where there had previously been excavation of gravel.

Members believed they could recover the plane, even after more than 55 years of mystery.

Bandleader Glenn Miller

11th August 1951: The first test flight of the largest commercial plane over California, the Lockheed Constellation

FLYING TIGER LINE FLIGHT 739, 1962

A Lockheed L-1049 Super Constellation, chartered by the US military to carry soldiers from California to Saigon, refuelled in Guam and was on its way to the Philippines when it disappeared without a trace or a distress signal.

Flying Tiger Line Flight 739, known as 21 Charlie, took off from Guam in the western Pacific for Clark Air Base in the Philippines on 16 March 1962. On board were 107 people, including 96 soldiers.

The flight disappeared over an abyss in the Pacific Ocean called the Mariana Trench, the deepest part of the Pacific said to be almost 7 miles to the bottom.

The disappearance of the Super Constellation prompted one of the largest air and sea searches in the history of the Pacific.

According to the US military publication Stars and Stripes, theories included sabotage, hijacking and even friendly fire.

The Civil Aeronautics Board never came up with a precise cause, and the wreckage was never discovered. The weather that night was good: broken cumulus clouds, no turbulence, and moonlit visibility of 15 miles.

The board eventually concluded that there was probably an in-flight explosion, based on a report from the crew of the tanker ship S/S T L Lenze that they saw an explosion in the sky in the general area where the plane was flying.

REPRESENTATIVES HALE BOGGS AND NICK BEGICH, 1972

On 16 October 1972 US House Majority Leader Hale Boggs, a Democrat from New Orleans, Louisiana, and Democrat Nick Begich, from Alaska, disappeared on a flight out of Anchorage, Alaska.

Boggs and Begich boarded a twin-engine Cessna in Anchorage but the plane vanished on its way to Juneau.

It was never found despite a 39-day search that The Washington Post called "the largest in Alaska history," involving more than 70 aircraft and 3,600 hours of flying time.

The 2 other people on board were Russell Brown, an aide to Nick Begich, and pilot Don Jonz.

The plane was thought to have gone down around the Chugach Mountains but no wreckage or bodies were found.

Hale Boggs was serving on the famous Warren Commission that was investigating the John F. Kennedy assassination. He was pushing for the case to be reopened, so it was not surprising that conspiracy theories arose.

VARIG BOEING 707-323C, 1979

A Boeing 707 cargo aircraft of Varig Brazilian Airlines disappeared on 30 January 1979, just 30 minutes after takeoff from Narita International Airport, Tokyo. The Rio-bound flight had 6 people on board.

The most interesting confirmed cargo was 153 of Manabu Mabe's paintings valued at more than $US 1.2 million.

A theory of a former employee of Varig has been put forward by his son and involves the defection in 1979 of a Soviet MiG pilot in Japan.

The MiG was the latest model and it would not have pleased the Soviets for it to fall into Western hands. The Soviets apparently put pressure on Japan to give the MiG back, but the US wanted it.

The theory, published on the *airliners.net* web site is that the US disassembled the MiG and decided to use a third-party foreign cargo carrier to take it to the US, rather than risk having the Soviets shoot down a Japanese plane (US ally) or US military plane and start a greater incident.

The plane was flying from Narita to Rio de Janeiro-Galeão via Los Angeles and was supposed to check in at regular intervals so maintenance, cargo and dispatcher groups would know when to be ready for a landing. There were no calls. The plane just disappeared.

No wreckage was found and the former Varig employee believed that was the preferred outcome so that the risk of someone finding out the MiG was onboard was eliminated.

The former employee, according to his son, had been in Brazil years later and asked what had happened to the plane to be told it had been shot down but all information was confidential.

Fact or fiction? Nothing is known for certain. The plane, people and paintings all remain missing.

IAN MACKINTOSH, RALLY 235, 1979

Ian Mackintosh, former Royal Navy officer and creator and writer of The Sandbaggers British television series, disappeared on 7 July 1979, just a few weeks short of his 39th birthday while on a flight over Alaska with his girlfriend Susan Insole and friend Graham Barber who was flying the single-engine Rally 235.

A distress signal was picked up by David Luedtke, aircraft traffic control specialist at the Federal Aviation Authority's (FAA) Kodiak airport, who alerted the US Coast Guard. But when a fixed wing Lockheed C-130 reached Barber's last reported position half an hour later, there was no trace of the plane, wreckage or any survivors. Over the next 18 hours 2 helicopters and another C-130 joined the search. A Coast Guard ship joined in and the search continued over the next few days. No evidence of the crash was found.

There were suspicions about the plane's disappearance.

Luedtke outlined his thoughts to American writer Robert Folsom, the author of a book on Inverness-born Mackintosh. Luedtke told of hearing about a State

Department official briefing Luedtke's boss that someone on the plane had set up a crash in order to defect.

It is a theory befitting a Mackintosh plot but family and friends believe it highly unlikely Mackintosh would have been defecting, even though he had worked in intelligence operations previously.

JOHN F. KENNEDY JR, 1999

Searchers took 4 days to find wreckage and another day to find the bodies of those on board the Piper Saratoga plane that crashed into the Atlantic Ocean off the coast of Martha's Vineyard, Massachusetts, on 16 July 1999.

The pilot, who died in the crash, was John F. Kennedy Jr, 38, son of President John F. Kennedy. Those who died with him were his wife, Carolyn Bessette, and sister-in-law, Lauren Bessette.

The flight left Essex County Airport, New Jersey, heading for Martha's Vineyard Airport along the coast of Connecticut and across Rhode Island Sound.

The plane was reported overdue at 10.05 pm on 16 July. Coast Guard searchers found the plane wreckage on the ocean floor on 20 July. Divers found Carolyn and Lauren's bodies near what was left of the fuselage. Kennedy's body was still strapped in the pilot's seat.

The National Transportation Safety Board found the crash was caused by "the pilot's failure to maintain control of the airplane during a descent over water at night, which was a result of spatial disorientation."

According to documentary maker John Hankey, the facts that Kennedy's plane inexplicably went straight into the ocean and that the fuel selector valve had been turned off suggested someone on board wanted to commit suicide.

According to documentary maker John Hankey, the facts that Kennedy's plane inexplicably went straight into the ocean and that the fuel selector valve had been turned off suggested someone on board wanted to commit suicide. There was also speculation that a fourth person was on the plane, but there were no witnesses to the boarding.

Questions were asked about why it took 15 hours to begin a search.

When it comes to Kennedy family incidents a conspiracy theory surely will follow.

One theory aired was that Kennedy Jr, a lawyer, journalist and magazine publisher, had told close associates he intended to run for the Senate from New York, and then for the Presidency. This, it is claimed, meant his political opponents wanted to remove him.

And 15 years later the gossip magazines were still speculating – that Kennedy Jr had wanted to leave his wife for a model; proving that the name Kennedy is also always good for a headline.

BOEING 727 TAIL NUMBER 844AA, 2003

Was it stolen to become a flying bomb for terrorists or was its disappearance part of an insurance scam?

Though an ageing plane, the former American Airlines Boeing 727-223 was fitted with all the modern instruments of the time. American engineer Ben Charles Padilla and his new Congolese assistant John Mikel Mutantu were working on the 727 at Quatro de Fevereiro, Luanda, Angola, on 25 May 2003, preparing it for its next flight.

While on lease to TAAG Angola Airlines, the 727 (tail number 844AA) had been grounded and sat idle at Luanda for 14 months accruing more than $US 4 million in backdated airport fees. It was one of 2 planes being converted for use by IRS Airlines from Abuja, Nigeria.

Neither engineer had a commercial pilot's license or permission to be in the cockpit.

The 28-year-old plane usually had a flight crew of 3 to fly it safely.

It is not known whether anyone else was on the plane when it suddenly started up, taxied and took off just before sunset. The headlights and transponders had been switched off and no one on board responded to calls from air traffic controllers.

Some reports said there was only one person on board the plane at the time; others suggested there may have been more than 2.

Authorities watched the jet head south-west towards the Atlantic Ocean. It was the last sighting of 844AA. Padilla's family has not heard anything from him since that day.

There was much speculation. Just two years after the 9/11 attacks in the US the war on terror was at its height so a popular theory was that 844AA had been hijacked for use by terrorists and the plane had been hidden somewhere as it was made ready for an attack. Others believed it could have landed at a remote airstrip and was being sold for parts.

A world-wide search by the American FBI and CIA and others over several months found nothing.

SPORTS ★ ★ ★ ★ FINAL

DAILY NEWS

$1.00   www.nycdailynews.com   **NEW YORK'S HOMETOWN NEWSPAPER**   Sunday, July 18, 1999

LOST

JFK Jr., wife presumed dead in plane crash off Vineyard

AMELIA EARHART
MISSED BY A FEW MILES

The disappearance of celebrated aviator Amelia Mary Earhart in 1937 is still the subject of speculation almost 80 years later. An ongoing search for her plane, and a successful global aerial circumnavigation of the world by namesake Amelia Rose Earhart, kept Amelia Mary Earhart's final flight in the spotlight

AMELIA EARHART, 1937

On a sunny morning, Friday 2 July 1937, a Lockheed Electra flew out of Lae airport in what is now Papua New Guinea on the second last leg of an around-the-world flight.

At the controls was world famous flyer Amelia Mary Earhart. Her navigator was the highly experienced Fred Noonan.

They were on their way to the tiny Pacific Island of Howland, the last scheduled stop (for fuel) before completing the last leg that would take them to their starting point in California, completing a record-breaking circumnavigation of the globe.

Amelia Earhart and Fred Noonan never made it to Howland Island, probably only falling short of their destination by a matter of minutes and miles.

But precisely where their plane crashed or crash-landed remains a mystery.

The dream of flying around the world in the twin-engine Electra was no flight of fantasy for such an experienced flyer as Amelia Earhart.

AMELIA EARHART'S RECORD:

- Woman's world altitude record: 14,000 ft (1922)
- First woman to fly the Atlantic (1928)
- Speed records for 100 km – and with cargo (1931)
- First woman to fly an autogyro (1931)
- Altitude record for autogyros: 15,000 ft (1931)
- First person to cross the US in an autogyro (1932)
- First woman to fly the Atlantic solo (1932)
- First person to fly the Atlantic twice (1932)
- First woman to receive the Distinguished Flying Cross (1932)
- First woman to fly nonstop, coast-to-coast across the U.S. (1933)
- Woman's speed transcontinental record (1933)
- First person to fly solo between Honolulu, Hawaii and Oakland, California (1935)
- First person to fly solo from Los Angeles, California to Mexico City, Mexico (1935)
- First person to fly solo nonstop from Mexico City, Mexico to Newark, New Jersey (1935)

She had failed at her first attempt at circumnavigation in March 1937 when a blown tyre damaged the plane on take-off from Hawaii. She had the plane shipped back to California for repair and prepared for another attempt.

It was the first all-metal plane and was modified for long distance with the 10 passenger seats replaced by 12 fuel tanks.

Amelia Earhart had chosen the longest route, 29,000 miles around the Equator. For the attempt, Lockheed Aircraft Company had built an Electra 10E to Earhart's specifications. It was the first all-metal plane and was modified for long distance with the 10 passenger seats replaced by 12 fuel tanks. The refitted plane had a theoretical range of 4,000 miles. It was an advanced aircraft for the time, with variable pitch propellers and retractable landing gear.

The Electra left Miami on 1 June 1937 with stops scheduled in South America, Africa, India and South East Asia. It arrived in Lae on 29 June 1937.

By then the Electra had travelled 22,000 miles, leaving about 7,000 miles to go over the Pacific Ocean.

HIGH RISKS

The flight from Lae to a refuelling stopover on Howland Island was to take 18 hours. The risks were high: Howland Island was only a mile wide, 2 miles long and 20 feet above sea level, a speck of land in the vast Pacific.

Bad weather, even cloud cover, would make the tiny island particularly hard to find.

So it was arranged that the American Coast Guard cutter Itasca would be on station at Howland to maintain radio contact and set off flares.

The US Navy auxiliary tug Ontario was stationed about halfway between Lae and Howland to keep lookout for the Electra.

They were to be the contact points for Earhart as she flew on a path just north of east to Howland and her final stopover.

Flying at about 134.5 mph ground speed, the Electra reported in from Nukumanu Islands, formerly Tasman Islands, a medium sized atoll in the south-western Pacific Ocean, south of the equator and about one-third of the way to Howland and about 6.5 hours into the flight. Everything was in order.

The fuel load on take-off at Lae had overloaded the Electra as Earhart ensured a sufficient supply to make

it to Howland. Strong headwinds may have increased consumption greater than expected, but by the half-way mark no alarm had been raised.

During the night Earhart reported seeing the lights of a ship below. It turned out to be the SS Myrtlebank on its way from Auckland, New Zealand, to Nauru. At that point, she still had around 1,140 miles to go.

She was still sending positional messages as she passed by the Gilbert Islands. At one point Itasca heard her report that conditions were partly cloudy as she came to within 4 hours of Howland.

The Electra descended below the clouds and headed for where Earhart and Noonan believed Howland Island would be.

GAS RUNNING LOW

A radio message to Itasca said "we must be on you but cannot see you but gas is running low, been unable reach you by radio we are flying at altitude 100 feet."

But the ship didn't respond.

A clue to the communications problem came later: photos and home movies at Lae appeared to show a radio antenna on the bottom of the plane breaking away as it taxied along the runway.

That could explain why Earhart was unable to hear Itasca's crew who were trying to contact her.

While the Electra should have been close to Howland

Island neither Earhart nor Noonan saw the Itasca and the ship never saw the plane.

It follows that those on the plane also never saw smoke put up to help them find the island.

Fuel would have been low, close to empty.

Earhart's last transmission was "we are running north and south."

The Electra had missed Howland Island and with no other significant land within 1,000 miles, logically it would have fallen in to the sea after running out of fuel.

The Itasca, bolstered by a crew from Howland Island, began searching for the Electra when it became obvious it was overdue. Having no success, a message was sent to American authorities including those at Pearl Harbour requesting a full scale search be launched. It was the biggest search for a plane at that time.

No confirmed trace of the plane or its occupants was found.

No confirmed trace of the plane or its occupants was found.

According to records, the official air and sea search by the US Navy and Coast Guard lasted until 19 July 1937.

A private search arranged by Amelia Earhart's husband George P. Putnam, an American publisher, author and explorer, also failed.

DEATH IN ABSENTIA

Putnam asked a probate court in Los Angles to have the usual "death in absentia" 7-year waiting period waived so that he could manage Earhart's finances. Earhart was declared legally dead on 5 January 1939.

Navigator and aeronautical engineer Elgen Long and his wife Marie K Long devoted 35 years of exhaustive research into the disappearance of Amelia Earhart.

They used long-lost radio messages, a great understanding of flight (Elgen was the first to fly solo around the world over both Poles) and information recorded at the time to piece together the Electra's last days.

Their results are recorded in the book, *Amelia Earhart, the mystery solved*, Simon & Schuster paperbacks, 1999.

In a detailed examination of the available facts, their conclusion is the logical one; that the Electra missed Howland Island, ran out of fuel and crashed into the sea.

FORCED LANDING?

Researchers at the International Group for Historic Aircraft Recovery (TIGHAR) believe Amelia Earhart's plane made a forced landing on Nikumaroro, or Gardner Island, part of the Phoenix Islands, Kiribati, in the western Pacific Ocean. It is a remote, elongated triangular heavily vegetated coral atoll 350 miles south-east of Howland Island.

TIGHAR's executive director, Richard Gillespie, and a crew have searched Nikumaroro extensively over many years.

Items recovered by TIGHAR have strengthened its view that it is looking in the right place.

Among the items was a small cosmetics jar, identified as probably a jar of Dr. Berry's Freckle Ointment, used to fade freckles. TIGHAR placed significance on this find as it was documented that Amelia Earhart disliked having freckles.

Other more substantial items recovered included a woman's shoe and a sextant box with serial numbers believed to be consistent with a type carried by Noonan.

Also recovered was a small piece of an aluminium panel which TIGHA now believes came from a repaired window on the Electra's fuselage which had not been noticed in pictures of the plane until 2014 when a photo taken before she took off for Puerto Rico on 1 June 1937 was examined more closely.

TIGHAR also says sonar readings of the ocean in the area are consistent with a large object on the ocean floor.

Gillespie believes Earhart landed on a coral reef just off Gardner Island and rough weather washed the plane off the reef into a deep ocean trough below. While Earhart and Noonan possibly made it ashore they would have eventually perished without food and water

THE THEORIES

In the vacuum of immediate knowledge of what happened to Earhart and Noonan rumours and conspiracy theories abounded.

According to *History.com*, some of the more fanciful theories that emerged over 75 years included:

- Landed on Saipan only to be executed by the Japanese.

- Flight was an elaborate scheme to spy on the Japanese, who captured her after she crashed.

- Survived a Pacific Ocean plane crash, was secretly repatriated to New Jersey and lived out her life under an assumed name.

- Survived and somehow made her way to Guadalcanal.

- Crashed on New Britain Island.

- Captured by the Japanese and became "Tokyo Rose."

- Captured by the Japanese and taken to Emirau Island in the Bismarck Archipelago, Papua New Guinea.

EARHART AGAIN

Amelia Earhart set out in June 2014 to fly around the globe in a single-engine turbo-prop plane

This isn't an old story re-circulated. This was a 31-year-old namesake, also a pilot.

On 12 July 2014 Amelia Rose Earhart completed the round-the-world flight that her namesake never finished nearly eight decades ago.

Amelia Rose and her co-pilot Shane Jordan took off from Oakland on June 26 and made 17 stops in 14 countries. They flew in a Pilatus PC-12 plane equipped with GPS and other modern technology her namesake never had.

She began her round-the-world flight from the same hangar used by Amelia Mary in 1937.

Amelia Rose wasn't always interested in flying. She said people who heard her name always asked her if she was a pilot. She eventually decided to give aviation a try.

Amelia Rose said she was embarrassed by the famous name her mother gave her, preferring to be called Amy.

She had thought for some time that she was a distant relative of the 1930s pilot. But that turned out not to be so. That didn't discourage Amelia Rose, who said it "taught me that Amelia and I share something much deeper than a genealogical connection... we share a spirit to soar."

"Amelia's disappearance unfortunately came at a time when the technology just wasn't there to track her. But when you think about how far that's come in the last 77 years, we're looking at a whole different world," she said.

"I started thinking, what if I could symbolically close Amelia's flight plan for her?"

Amelia Rose, a weather and traffic reporter by profession, had been a pilot for 10 years. Until 2014 her longest solo flight was from Switzerland to Colorado.

She said she hoped her global flight would inspire girls to fly. She started a non-profit Fly With Amelia Foundation, to enable teenage girls to attend flight school.

Amelia Rose's flight path took her over Howland Island near where Amelia Mary disappeared.

"We just circled Howland Island. I've always respected AE and her bravery," she tweeted on July 9, "but seeing this tiny island takes it to a whole new level."

Her hands shook, not from fear, she said, but from forging a deeper connection with her namesake while flying over the atoll in the central Pacific Ocean where the original Earhart disappeared.

A CENTURY OF MYSTERY

CECIL GRACE AND THE CHANNEL, 1910 TO 1944

Several planes have disappeared over the English Channel; the first recorded being the loss of a Short S27 and its pilot, Cecil Grace, on 22 December 1910 on a flight from Calais to Dover.

Grace, an Irish-American whose uncle, W R Grace, had been a mayor of New York, began his flying career out of Eastchurch, on the island of Sheppey, with members of the Aero Club of Great Britain, formed in 1909.

He was a star attraction at the first air show held in Ireland in August 1910 but his major challenge that year was the De Forest Prize. The competition was to leave England from anywhere in the country and after crossing the Channel fly in a straight line as far into Europe as possible. The prize was 4,000 pounds.

According to the Kent History Forum, Cecil Grace was flying a Short S27 which had been modified by Oswald Short to include flotation bags in case the pilot had to ditch in the sea. But Grace had decided that fuel load was more important than the heavy flotation bags and removed them. He had also abandoned his compass which he had found to be cumbersome and unreliable.

Grace flew over the Channel and reached Calais but the headwind had increased so much that he was barely making any headway. He decided to abandon the attempt that day and return to Eastchurch via Dover and try again the next day. On the return journey the wind dropped and a fog formed. About mid-afternoon the crew of the North Goodwin Lightship heard the engine of a plane fly over but it seemed to be heading out over the North Sea. That was the last recorded report of Grace's position.

Grace apparently wore a cork jacket which he had believed could keep him afloat for an indefinite period. In January 1911 a pilot's goggles and a cap were washed up on the shore at Mariakerk, Belgium, and identified as belonging to Cecil Grace.

Others listed as disappearing on flights over the Channel

include: A Morane-Saulnier monoplane and Gustav Hamel on 23 May 1914; a Fokker T.III on a delivery flight from Amsterdam to London on 15 November 1924; An Armstrong Whitworth Atlas military patrol with two people aboard on 27 March 1931; A Handley Page HP45 Harrow with three people aboard on a night military training flight during a storm on 6 October 1938; and A UC-64 Norseman military transport with three people aboard, including band leader Glenn Miller, on a flight from Clapham to Paris on 15 December 1944.

ÉDOUARD JEAN BAGUE, 1911, AND OTHERS

French Aviator Édouard Jean Bague wanted to be the first to fly a plane across the Mediterranean Sea.

His first attempt came up short. In March 1911 he planned to fly from Antibes to Ajaccio, Corsica; from there to Sardinia and then via Sicily to Tunis. But he miscalculated and landed instead on the small Italian island of Gorgona, 120 miles from his starting point. His Blériot XI monoplane was damaged and Bague was injured.

But he didn't give up.

In the early morning of 5 June 1911, around 5 o'clock and with a few friends watching, Bague, 32, set off in a monoplane equipped with floats, "just in case". He intended to fly from Nice to Tunis via Corsica, Sardinia and Sicily.

The Nice to Valvi leg was just less than 120 miles. Bague's plane disappeared after leaving Nice. Navy ships were dispatched to search for him and a witness reported seeing a plane apparently in difficulty in the area. Bague and his plane were never seen again. One report said Bague had not taken a compass with him.

Blériot monoplanes of various kinds claimed two more lives in the next two years, disappearing without trace: Irish-born Damer Leslie Allen disappeared on 18 April 1912 while trying to fly from Holyhead, Wales, to Ireland. American Albert Jewell disappeared off Long Island, New York, on 13 October 1913 on his way to Oakwood, Staten Island, for the New York Times American Aerial Derby.

GUSTAV HAMEL, 1914

Gustav Hamel was prominent in the early history of aviation in Britain. He pioneered mail deliveries by air and gave several flying displays that included taking a female passenger to be the first to experience a Loop-the-Loop.

In 1911 Hamel flew a Blériot the 21 miles between Hendon and Windsor in 10 minutes to deliver the first official airmail to the Postmaster General.

On 23 May 1914, he disappeared over the English Channel while returning from Paris in a new 80 hp Morane-Saulnier monoplane he had just collected.

THE ATLANTIC, 1927 TO 1939

Early attempts to cross the Atlantic claimed many aircraft and flyers.

According to Wikipedia, the list includes: The White Bird Levassuer PL.8 with two people aboard which disappeared on 8 May 1927 trying to be the first to cross from Paris to New York; a Fokker F.VII, Old Glory, with three people aboard which disappeared over the North Atlantic on 7 September 1927 on a flight from Maine, US, to Rome,

Italy; A Sikorsky S-36, The Dawn, with four people on board which disappeared over the North Atlantic on 23 December 1927 on the way from New York to Newfoundland ; a Stinson SM-1 Detroiter, Endeavour, which disappeared on 13 March 1928 between Crookhaven and Newfoundland on an east to west flight that began in Cranwell, England; and a Ryan C-2 Foursome with two people aboard which disappeared over the North Atlantic on 11 August 1939 on a flight from St Peters, Nova Scotia, to Ireland.

NORTH SEA, 1928 TO 1939

The inhospitable North Sea has claimed more than its share of aircraft, disappeared and presumed lost in the sea.

The first recording of a plane disappearing there was a Blackburn R-1 with 3 people aboard that disappeared on a military reconnaissance mission on 6 September 1928.

Another 6 disappeared over the North Sea in less than two years: A Vickers Wellesley attempting an around-Britain flight with three people aboard on 24 February 1938; a Hawker Hector and pilot on a military navigation flight on 6 August 1938; An Avro Anson on a military flight with four people aboard on 8 August 1938; A Westland Wallace military tow

9th September 1911: Gustav Hamel gets ready for take-off in a Bleriot monoplane to deliver mail from Hendon to Windsor

Inset: Pioneer aviator Gustav Hamel posting the letter at Hendon, which he carried himself to Windsor in the first aerial postal delivery

plane with two people aboard over a firing range on 9 May 1939; A Vickers Wellington I with five people aboard on a military flight from REAF Mildenhall on 9 August 1939; and a Supermarine Stranger on a military patrol with six people on board between Scotland and Norway on 19 August 1939.

SOUTHERN CLOUD, 1931

The Southern Cloud, a 3-engine Avro 618 Ten plane from Australian National Airways, took off from Mascot airport in Sydney, Australia, bound for Melbourne on 21 March 1931 with 2 crew and 6 passengers.

Three hours after it left Sydney a weather report warned of severe storm activity and gales along the route. But the Southern Cloud did not have a radio.

The plane didn't make it to Melbourne and there were no clues as to its disappearance.

The search for the missing plane continued for 18 days. The searchers included airline co-owner and renowned aviator Charles Kingsford Smith. Nothing was found.

But 27 years later, on 26 October 1958, Tom Sonter, a carpenter on the Snowy Mountains Hydro-electric Scheme, saw what he thought was the remains of an old mining shaft and went to investigate. What he had spotted turned out to be the wreckage of a plane, later identified as the Southern Cloud.

GW SALT AND FB TAYLOR, 1932

English planters GW Salt and FB Taylor went missing in their Avro 616 Avian IVM plane over the Gulf of Martaban in southern Burma on 12 August 1932.

They were flying from Moulmein (Mawlamyine) to Rangoon (Yangon) in Burma, and eventually on to England.

Their plane, G-AAKA, is believed to have crashed into the sea. Wreckage was spotted a month later in the Gulf of Martaban but it was never confirmed as the planters' plane.

LATÉCOÈRE 301, 1936

The Air France flying boat Ville de Buenos Aires disappeared with 6 people on board in February 1936 on a flight from Natal, Brazil, to Dakar, French West Africa. After a radio message from near Saint Peter and Saint Paul Archipelago reporting it was flying in rain at 300 metres, nothing more was ever heard of the plane.

Aboard was Émile Barrière, an early twentieth-century French aviator.

Another Latécoère 301, with 5 people on board, disappeared in December that year. It was being flown by another Frenchman, Jean Mermoz, who was also a pioneer aviator recognised for his deeds in Argentina and Brazil as well as France.

BOLKHOVITINOV DBA, 1937

The DB-A heavy long-range bomber was designed by Viktor Fedorovich Bolkhovitinov and built in the USSR from 1934.

After successful initial testing it was decided to fly the plane non-stop from Moscow to the US.

The red DB-A prototype under command of Sigizmund Levanevsky left Moscow Shchyelkovo Airport on 12 August 1937 for Fairbanks, Alaska.

The crew sent a radio message that one engine had failed and gave a revised arrival time at Fairbanks, but nothing further was heard from the DB-A and crew of 6.

ANDREW CARNEGIE WHITFIELD, 1938

Andrew Carnegie Whitfield, nephew of American steel magnate Andrew Carnegie, disappeared in his silver and red Taylor Cub plane on 17 April 1938. Visibility was clear and the weather good. He was flying from Roosevelt Field, Long Island, New York, to the nearby town of Brentwood, New York. His plane disappeared near Norwalk Island, New York.

The lack of any plane wreckage raised suspicions and it was discovered that on the day he vanished, he had checked into a hotel in Garden City on Long Island under an alias he occasionally used, "Albert C. White."

When the hotel room was opened his personal belongings, clothing, cuff links engraved with his initials, two life insurance policies, and several stock and bond certificates had been left there. Phone records also indicated that he had called his home while his family was out looking for him.

Police then formed the view Whitfield had committed suicide by flying his plane into the Atlantic Ocean, even though there was no direct evidence. There was no indication Whitfield was having personal or business problems.

HAWAII CLIPPER, 1938

The Hawaii Clipper, one of three Martin M-130 commercial flying boats built in 1935, was designed to meet Pan American Airway's requirement for trans-Pacific luxury aircraft. In July 1938, Hawaii Clipper Flight 229 carrying 9 crew and 6 passengers, was flying from Alameda, California, to Manila by way of Honolulu, Midway, Wake, and Guam. The last radio contact put the Hawaii Clipper 565 miles from the Philippine coast. It was not heard of again.

The passenger list included 2 distinguished men: Dr. Earl Baldwin McKinley, Dean of Medicine at George Washington University, and Dr. Fred C. Meier, plant pathologist of the

Department of Agriculture, who were en route from Guam to Manila in search of the answer to the puzzle of the trans-oceanic spread of disease germs and plant pollen.

According to reports some time later, the Hawaii Clipper was carrying $3m in US currency. A New Jersey Chinese-born restaurateur, Wah Sun "Watson" Choy, was carrying this cash in his role as President of the Chinese War Relief Committee. The money came from fundraising in the US to be given to the Chinese government.

IMPERIAL AIRWAYS HANDLEY PAGE HP42, 1940

On a trip to the United Kingdom from India, an Imperial Airways Handley Page HP42E disappeared without trace on 1 March 1940 with 8 on board. One of the passengers was World War I flying ace Air Commodore Harold A. Whistler, DFC, DSO, Chief of Air Staff RAF India.

The Handley Page HP42E "Hannibal" departed from its eastern base at Karachi Drigh Road airfield at sunrise. Six hours later it departed after refuelling from Jiwani, Pakistan, and headed out over the Gulf of Oman. It was never seen again

DOUGLAS C-54 SKYMASTER, 1944

Decorated soldier Lt col. Leon Robert "Bob" Vance Jr who served in the US Army Air Force during World War II was one of a group of wounded soldiers who boarded a C-54 Skymaster transport plane in England for the trip home on 26 July 1944.

The Skymaster disappeared somewhere between Iceland and Newfoundland. No trace of it or the people on board were found.

Vance had been one of 12 airmen aboard the B-24 Liberator Missouri Sue for a raid by the 489th Bombardment Group on targets at Wimereaux on 5 June 1944, the day before D-Day. The Missouri Sue's bombs didn't release on the first pass so they tried again but ran into a stream of anti-aircraft fire and the plane and some crew members were hit.

PAN-AMERICAN AIRWAYS "CHINA CLIPPER" ARRIVES AT SAN FRANCISCO, FROM THE ORIENT

© CLYDE SUNDERLAND

The Handley Page HP42 (behind the light aircraft) by the British Imperial Airways was the biggest airplane in the world at that time

Inset: The Handley Page HP42 was the most famous Imperial Airways airliner of the period

The captain took a fatal hit and Vance who had been riding as an observer took over the controls, even though his foot had been almost severed by shrapnel. But the damage to the plane was catastrophic (all engines were out) and the order to "bail out" was given as the plane glided towards England.

Ten men parachuted out. Vance was stuck at the controls by his damaged foot and a bomb that had not released was still on board.

As the bomb would explode in a crash, Vance guided the plane away from land for a water crash-landing. A British crew rescued Vance and another crewman who had stayed on board. Vance came-to in hospital where his foot was finally amputated.

He had been told he'd been nominated for the Medal of Honour before he boarded the flight home where he was to be fitted with an artificial foot. On 4 January 4 1945, Vance was awarded the medal posthumously. Vance Air Force base near Enid, Oklahoma, is named for him.

THE COMMANDO, 1945

A B-24 Liberator nicknamed Commando, formerly the personal transport of Winston Churchill, disappeared near the Azores on 27 March 1945 and all aboard were presumed lost.

The plane was carrying dignitaries from England to Canada for a ceremony marking the closure of the Empire Air Training Scheme.

Among them was Air Marshal Sir Peter Roy Maxwell Drummond KCB, DSO & Bar, OBE, MC, an Australian-born senior commander in the Royal Air Force.

AVRO LANCASTRIAN, 1946

The Australian airline Qantas has an impeccable safety record in its jet fleet. But there have been a dozen incidents through its history involving propeller planes.

An Avro 691 Lancastrian operated by Qantas and leased from British Overseas Airways Corporation vanished over the Indian Ocean on 23 March 1946 on a flight from Karachi via Sri Lanka (then Ceylon) to Australia via Cocos Islands, a total flight distance of 1,776 miles. There were 10 people aboard, including a Qantas crew.

LATÉCOÈRE 631, 1948

A gigantic Latécoère 631 flying boat of Air France went missing over the Atlantic Ocean on 2 August 1984 with 52 people on board on a flight from Fort de France, Martinique, to Port-Etienne, French West Africa. It was last heard of 1,200 miles off the Dakar African coast. The search mounted in the South Atlantic was one of the biggest at that time and included the US Coast Guard cutter Campbell which reported finding debris that could have been from the plane.

The accident led to the withdrawal of the Latécoère 631 planes from service by Air France.

BRITISH SOUTH AMERICAN AIRWAYS PLANES, 1948-1949

Two planes operated by British South American Airways (BSAA) vanished without a trace while flying in the Caribbean.

Avro Tudor G-AHNP Star Tiger was carrying 31 people on a flight from Portugal to Bermuda on 30 January 1948 when it disappeared from radars over the Atlantic Ocean not long after a fuel stop in Santa Maria.

While it took off into heavy rain and strong winds, the plane - which had come into service only two months earlier - stayed in radio contact behind another plane travelling the same route in fine weather.

However, it failed to arrive in Bermuda. A British investigation into the disappearance concluded "the fate of Star Tiger must remain an unsolved mystery".

Less than a year later, on 17 January 1949, another BSAA Avro Tudor G-AGRE Star Ariel went missing with 20 people on board while flying from Bermuda to Jamaica in perfect conditions.

An investigation into that disappearance concluded: "through lack of evidence due to no wreckage having been found, the cause of the accident is unknown".

DOUGLAS DC-3 1948

A Douglas DC-3 Airborne Transport (DST) left San Juan Airport, Puerto Rico, on 28 December 1948.

When the plane contacted New Orleans it reported its position as 45 miles from Miami, but it was later thought the pilot may have been mistaken.

The plane, its 29 passengers and three crew members were never found and its disappearance has sometimes been included in those attributed to the Bermuda Triangle. Before the final flight there had been some electrical problems with the plane.

DOUGLAS SKYMASTER, 1950

A Douglas C-54D Skymaster, operated by the US Air Force and designated as USAF Flight 2469, disappeared flying from Anchorage, Alaska, to Great Falls, Montana, on the way to El Paso, Texas, with 44 people aboard on 26 January 1950. The passengers included a pregnant woman and her infant son. The passengers were fitted with parachutes.

The plane disappeared somewhere over the Yukon, near Snag. More than 80 aircraft took part in the search for the missing plane. The Royal Canadian Mounted Police received many reports of witnesses seeing an aircraft in distress and of hearing a crash and seeing smoke.

Search efforts were hampered by heavy ice conditions and snowstorms. But months of searching on land and from the air did not find the plane or the people aboard.

The Avro Tudor 8, jet version of the Tudor series of aircraft. Powered by four Rolls Royce Nene turbojet engines.

NORTHWEST ORIENT AIRLINES FLIGHT 2501, 1950

Northwest Orient Airlines Flight 2501 took off from New York's LaGuardia Airport on the evening of 23 June 1950 bound for Seattle, Washington, via Minneapolis. The plane with 55 passengers and 3 crew disappeared. It is believed the DC-4 still sits somewhere on the bottom of Lake Michigan.

The plane was passing over Battle Creek, Michigan when the pilot, Captain Robert C. Lind, told the tower he expected to be over Milwaukee in 45 minutes. The plane was at 3,500 feet when it entered a storm approaching Lake Michigan.

Lind asked permission to drop to 2,500 feet but his request was denied due to traffic in the area. That was the last communication.

The US Navy, Coast Guard and police from Wisconsin, Michigan, and Illinois searched Lake Michigan after reports of oil slicks. Debris including seat cushions, clothing, blankets and a fuel tank float was found 10 miles off the shore of South Haven, Michigan. Human remains were located but no intact bodies. The search was called off after four days.

The cause of the plane's disappearance was never determined.

C-124 TRANSPORT, 1951

A Douglas C-124 Globemaster II operated by the United States Air Force disappeared on 23 March 1951 after a fire forced the pilots to ditch in the Atlantic Ocean off the coast of Shannon, Ireland.

The plane was flying from Limestone-Loring Air Force Base after a refueling stop in Maine, in the US, to Lackenheath RAF base with 53 people, including senior Air Force personnel, on board.

The aircraft apparently landed on the water safely and intact with those on board donning life preservers and climbing into inflatable rafts. The rafts were equipped with survival supplies including food, water, signal flares, cold-weather gear, and "Gibson Girl" hand crank emergency radios.

The rafts and flares were spotted by another aircraft but when rescuers arrived at the scene 19 hours later, there was no sign of the plane, people or survival equipment. All that was found was some charred wood and a briefcase.

There was speculation at the time that the crew may have been taken by a Soviet submarine believed to be operating in the area.

CANADIAN PACIFIC AIRLINES, 1951

A Douglas DC-4 of Canadian Pacific Airlines took off from Vancouver airport bound for Tokyo on 21 July 1951 with 31 passengers and 6 crew to assist in evacuations as the Korean War raged.

Its position was last recorded by the British Columbia Space Centre four hours after its departure from Vancouver.

The plane encountered rain, low visibility and icing conditions as it approached Anchorage, Alaska, but gave no indication of difficulties. No more was heard and a search by the US Air Force and the Royal Canadian Air Force over several months found no trace of the plane or those aboard.

F-89C SCORPION, 1953

A US interceptor F-89 Scorpion jet and crew of 2 disappeared on 23 November 1952 on a flight out of Kinross Air Base, Michigan.

Air Defense Command Ground Intercept radar operators at Sault Ste. Marie, Michigan, detected an unusual object near the Soo Locks and the Scorpion was scrambled, flown by First Lieutenant Felix Moncla with Second Lieutenant Robert L. Wilson as radar operator.

Ground radar tracked the plane and the other object as they drew closer. The two blips merged into one as if they collided. The second plane, according to investigators was a Canadian Air Force Dakota C-47 flying from Winnipeg to Sudbury, Canada, but the Canadians denied their plane was involved. There were no reports of another plane being involved in a crash.

A search and rescue operation failed to find a trace of the Scorpion or the crew.

SKYWAYS AVRO YORK, 1953

An Avro York four-engine airliner registered G-AHFA of Skyways Limited disappeared over the North Atlantic on a trooping flight from the United Kingdom to Jamaica on 2 February 1953. The plane, a civilian transport version of the Lancaster bomber, was carrying 39 occupants including 13 children. It had been chartered by the British Air Ministry.

Six hours after its departure from Lajes Field in the Azores for Gander airport in Newfoundland, Gander received a distress message then lost contact. A large search did not find any trace of the plane.

An inquest in London heard that the outstanding feature of the inquiry was the lack of evidence. No conclusion was reached but investigators recommended tighter maintenance checks and measures to combat crew fatigue.

AVRO SHACKELTONS, 1955

Two Avro Schackelton four-engine maritime patrol planes of No. 42 Squadron of the RAF disappeared off Fastnet Rock on the south-west Irish coast on 11 January 1955.

It is believed the 2 planes with a crew of 18 collided during their patrolling exercise. Routine radio transmissions indicated that they were flying at the prescribed separation (85 miles) during the night. But suddenly all contact was lost.

A 3-day search found nothing. In 1966, the starboard outer engine of one of the planes was recovered about 75 miles north of where authorities had long assumed the collision had occurred.

BROKEN ARROW B-47, 1956

A US Air Force B-47 Stratojet with 3 officers and the cores for 2 nuclear weapons on board disappeared on 10 March 1956 on a flight from MacDill Air Force Base in Florida.

The plane was one of a flight of 4 on a non-stop deployment from MacDill to an undisclosed overseas air base.

Crossing the Atlantic, the B-47s met a KC-97 Stratotanker flying from a temporary duty station in the Azores for their first aerial refueling. The second refueling was scheduled over the Mediterranean Sea.

The tanker was waiting for the planes under the cloud cover to make the refueling in clear weather. But just 3 of the B-47s emerged from the clouds. The fourth was missing. It was last reported near Sebatna in French Morocco.

Some witnesses reported seeing the bomber explode in the air over the desert to the south-east of Port Say, a small village along the Algerian coast near the Moroccan border.

An extensive search failed to locate any traces of the missing aircraft or three-man crew.

The loss of the weapons is referred to by Strategic Air Command as a "Broken Arrow".

PAN AM FLIGHT 7, 1957

On the afternoon of 8 November 1957, Pan American Airlines Clipper *Romance of the Skies* disappeared over the ocean halfway between San Francisco and Honolulu. The pilot's last transmission, at 5:04 pm local time, indicated all was well with the giant Boeing 377 Stratocruiser setting out on a luxury around-the-world aerial cruise with 44 people on board.

It is recorded on *romanceoftheskies.com* that among the passengers were the president of Renault Europe, an Air Force intelligence officer bound for Vietnam, a sailor returning to Tokyo to marry the Japanese woman he had met during the war, and a passenger who bought 3 large life insurance policies in the days before the flight. Romance was also carrying some unusual cargo: one of IBM's first computers, a shipment of radioactive isotopes, and 400 pounds of highly-flammable celluloid film.

The cause of the crash remains a mystery; no distress calls were received, the debris was far off course and toxicology reports revealed that several of the recovered bodies had high levels of carbon monoxide in their systems.

US AIR FORCE C-97C, 1957

A US Air Force Boeing C-97C-35-BO Stratofreighter disappeared in a storm 200 miles south-east of Tokyo, Japan, while on a flight from Travis Air Force Base to Tokyo on 22 March 1957.

There were 10 crew and 57 passengers on board. The plane is believed to have gone down in a storm 200 miles south-east of Tokyo. It was the deadliest incident involving a C-97.

BLUE GOOSE, 1958

The wreckage of a plane missing for 56 years was found in 2014 by fishermen in the Taiwan Strait, close to where the plane was thought to have crashed.

The plane, an amphibious PBY-5A nicknamed the Blue Goose, was carrying 11 US servicemen and 4 Taiwanese civilian crew members when it disappeared in October 1958. Wreckage was found in February 2014, according to the China Times.

The plane lost contact in the Taiwan Strait's 15-mile wide "no radar zone" flying at 1,000 feet to avoid Chinese radar.

At the time, the US had been assisting the Taiwanese military in its conflict with China after the Chinese military bombed several islands surrounding Taiwan and threatened to invade.

LOCKHEED SUPER CONSTELLATION, 1958

A Lockheed WV-2 Super Constellation operated by the US Navy disappeared over the North Atlantic on 20 February 1948 with 22 people on board.

The plane was on radar patrol, west of Ilha do Corvo, Azores, flying out of the Naval Air Station Argentia, Newfoundland and Labrador, to Lajes Field, Terceira Island, Azores.

MARTIN PBM-5 MARINER, 1958

A Martin Mariner seaplane operated by ARTOP disappeared south-west of Lisbon on a flight from Lisbon to Madeira on 9 November 1958 with 36 people aboard.

In the last radio contact, about an hour after take-off, the crew radioed: "I am forced to land immediately".

GULF AVIATION DC-3, 1960

A Gulf Aviation Douglas DC-3 disappeared on a flight from Bahrain to Sharjah via Doha on 10 July 1960. The plane with 16 people aboard did not reach Sharjah after taking off from Doha, No wreckage was found.

The pilot of a de Havilland Heron approaching Sharjah at the same time reported hearing the DC-3 crew trying to contact Sharjah. The calls were not heard by Sharjah but the interception of them near its expected arrival time and the strength of the tailwind on the route may indicate that the plane overflew Sharjah in bad visibility.

GARUDA INDONESIA FLIGHT 542, 1961

Garuda Indonesia Flight 542, a Douglas C-47A, disappeared off Madura Island on a scheduled domestic passenger flight from Surabaya-Juanda to Sultan Aji Muhamad Sulaiman

on the Indonesian Island of Kalimantan on 3 February 1961.

Five crew and 21 passengers were on board. No wreckage was found.

AVION PIRATA, 1961

The Lockheed Constellation referred to by Bolivians as Avion Pirata (pirate airplane) is still in Bolivia where it was forced to land by the Bolivian Air Force. But what it was doing and how the crew escaped is a mystery.

The plane was seen flying into El Trompillo Airport in Santa Cruz on 29 July 1961, but its cargo and operators were unknown, although it is widely believed to have been engaged in smuggling contraband from Panama to Bolivia, Brazil, Paraguay, Argentina and Uruguay.

It was forced to land under fire by 2 Bolivian Mustang fighters in July 1961. One of the fighters crashed, killing the pilot.

The Lockheed crew members, identified as pilots William Ray Robinson and William Friedman, co-pilot Salvatore Henrique Romano, flight engineer Bertrand Vinson and radio-man Gene Hawkins, were arrested.

In November 1961, it was revealed that the crew had escaped from Bolivia. They were tried in absentia and in 1967 prosecutors asked for 10 years imprisonment for each crew-

member. But none of the five men on the plane went back to Bolivia and their whereabouts remained unclear.

The "arrested" plane was put on display at Boris Banzer Prada Park, Santa Cruz, Bolivia. Reportedly it was at one time used as a brothel until residents complained, then a bank and a library. In 2000 it was painted in the colours of Pepsi as a billboard, a use that continued for various advertisers and local authorities.

DOUGLAS DC-4, 1964

A Douglas DC-4 operated by Facilities Management Corp disappeared at sea on 28 March 1964 after leaving Honolulu International Airport for Los Angeles with 9 people on board. It was said to be the plane used in the filming of The High and the Mighty.

Just under 4 hours from its expected arrival time flight controllers heard a "Mayday" call from the pilot who said the plane had a serious fire in number 2 and that "...we may have to put it in."

A five-day search by the United States Coast Guard, crew and planes from the aircraft carrier USS Kearsarge and other ships found no trace of the plane or those on board.

Investigations revealed the number 2 engine had a recurring oil leak in its propeller assembly on an earlier flight.

FUERZA AÉREA ARGENTINA C-54, 1965

Fuerza Aérea Argentina C-54, a Douglas C-54 Skymaster leased by the Argentine military, disappeared with 68 people on board on 1 November 1965.

The crew issued a distress call saying they would divert to Puerto Limon, Costa Rica, but nothing more was heard.

Investigators recovered 25 lifebuoys, personal belongings and some wreckage in the Bocas del Toro Archipelago.

The plane may have crashed into the dense Costa Rican jungle or into the Caribbean Sea but the precise location of the wreckage and its passengers remains unknown.

PLANE HIJACKING, 1969

North Korea is still believed to be holding somewhere 4 crew and 7 passengers from a Korean Airlines NAMC YS-11 hijacked on 11 December 1969. They are also still holding the plane.

The plane was on a domestic flight from Gangneung Airbase in Gangneung, Gangwon-do, to Gimpo International Airport, Seoul.

A North Korean agent, later identified as Cho Chang-hui, entered the cockpit and forced the pilots to fly into North Korean airspace. They were met by North Korean fighter jets and forced to land at Sŏndŏk Airfield near Wonsan.

North Korea released 39 passengers in February 1970 after subjecting them to indoctrination into North Korean politics.

Statements provided by released passengers refuted North Korea's claims that the hijacking was led by the pilots; they identified a passenger as the hijacker. A man on the plane said he sneaked a look out the window of the aircraft and saw the hijacker being driven away in a black car. Another passenger was reported to have become mentally deranged as a result of his captivity, and lost the ability to speak.

A mother of one of the flight attendants being held was allowed to visit her daughter in 2000 but the daughter remained in North Korea.

RIVET AMBER, 1969

A Boeing RC-136 reconnaissance plane, the Rivet Amber, was off the Kamchatka Peninsula on 5 June 1969 when it disappeared with 19 people on board. The plane is believed to have crashed into the Bering Sea, 240 miles off Shemaya, on a flight to Fairbanks for routine maintenance.

Just over half an hour after takeoff the Rivet Amber sent a radio message that it was "experiencing severe vibrations... going on oxygen and descending."

More than 3 weeks of searching found no trace of the plane or those on board.

ARIA 331, 1971

Twelve US Air Force personnel and 12 civilians were on a C-135 aircraft, Aria 331, that disappeared on 13 June 1971, returning to Hawaii after monitoring French nuclear testing in the Pacific in a classified operation called "Project III".

The plane was flying from Pago Pago, American Samoa, to Hickam Air Force Base in Hawaii and was last plotted 70 miles south of Hawaii near Palmyra Island.

A search began when the plane failed to reach Hickam by its estimated arrival time. It left Pago Pago 5 hours earlier with enough fuel for 9 hours flying.

A 1982 compensation case was told wreckage from the aircraft was recovered 700 miles south-west of Honolulu but no bodies were found. The court noted that the cause of the crash remained a mystery.

TAM-52, 1974

A Douglas DC-4 operated by Transporte Aereo Militar, the civilian branch of the Bolivian Air Force, disappeared on a non-scheduled passenger flight from Santa Rosa de Yacuma Airport to El Alto International Airport in La Paz on 10 January 1974. No trace of the aircraft, its 3 crew or 21 passengers has ever been found. The direct flight distance from Santa Rosa Airport to La Paz-El Alto Airport is 193 miles.

DC-4s have been involved in more than 300 major incidents and more than 3200 fatalities.

WEATHERBIRD, 1974

An American Lockheed WC-130H Weatherbird, also known as a "Hurricane Hunter," attached to the 54th Weather Reconnaissance Squadron and with the flight name Swan 38, was on its way to investigate Hurricane Bess on 12 October 1974 when it went it disappeared over the South China Sea.

The tracking plane left Clark Air Base in the Philippines and was believed to have been near the typhoon's eye when it lost radio contact.

The plane and its crew of 6, based at the 54th Weather Reconnaissance Squadron in Guam, were never found.

SAETA FLIGHT 232, 1976

A Vickers Viscount 785D from Ecuador carrying 55 passengers and 4 crew disappeared on a flight from Quito to Cuenca in Uruguay on 15 August 1976.

Wreckage was found many years later, in 2002, by climbers on Chimborazo Mountain and in 2003 it was confirmed as being SAETA flight 232. No reason for the crash was established but hijacking was suspected.

ARGOSY AIRLINES DC-3, 1978

An Argosy Airlines DC-3 left Fort Lauderdale in the US for Havana, Cuba, on 21 September 1978 with 4 people on board. It was to collect 21 citrus growers who had been touring Cuba. The plane disappeared off radar shortly after reaching cruising level off Fort Lauderdale. To believers, the Bermuda Triangle had claimed another victim.

Pilot George Hamilton had obtained special permission for the flight as Cuba was restricted territory. The others on board included his wife Barbara as flight attendant.

An hour after take-off, Argosy 902 was ready for approach to Havana. Suddenly it disappeared from radar. There was no SOS or "may day".

The plane had 32 yellow life jackets and the seat cushions were floatable. Coast Guard searchers found nothing and the search was called off two days later.

FLIGHT 191, 1979

A number of incidents involving flights numbered 191 have occurred over the years; so many that some airlines have done away with the flight number 191, like hotels that don't have a 13th floor.

The worst incident was American Airlines Flight 191, a regularly scheduled passenger flight from O'Hare International Airport in Chicago to Los Angeles International Airport.

The McDonnell Douglas DC-10 crashed on 25 May 1979 after takeoff from Chicago. All 258 passengers and 13 crew on board were killed, along with two people on the ground.

Investigators found that as the jet was beginning its takeoff rotation, engine number one on the left (port) wing separated and flipped over the top of the wing, leading to catastrophic failures that brought the plane down.

What has been noted is that since the 1960s, five flights with the number "191" have ended in fatal crashes, three of them in the US involving passenger planes, including the 1979 one.

BRITTEN-NORMAN ISLANDER, 1983

Seven people on a hunting trip are believed to have perished when a Britten-Norman 2A-21 Islander disappeared near Smithers, British Columbia, Canada, on 2 September 1983.

Among those on board was George Cogar, 51, inventor of the data recorder magnetic tape encoder, which was introduced in 1965 and eliminated the need for keypunches and punched cards by direct encoding on tape.

An extensive search failed to find the plane or the occupants.

UPALI AIR FLIGHT N482U, 1983

Upali Air flight N482U disappeared on 13 February 1983, 20 km off Kuala Selangor, Malaysia, in the Straits of Malacca.

The Learjet 35A was flying from Kuala Lumpur in Malaysia to Colombo-Katunayake, Sri Lanka, carrying 3 crew and 3 passengers. One of those aboard was Sri Lankan multi-millionaire businessman Upali Wijewardene.

The last radio contact was 15 minutes after takeoff when the pilot reported he was climbing. The pilot was supposed to contact Medan but no call was received.

A survival pack, believed to be from the Learjet, was found a few days later but nothing was seen again of the plane or those on board.

PITTS S-2, ART SCHOLL, 1985

A Pitts S-2 failed to recover from a flat spin and disappeared into the Pacific Ocean off Southern California in 1985 while filming the movie *Top Gun*. The pilot was Art (Arthur) Scholl, an American aerobatic pilot, aerial cameraman, flight instructor and educator.

Scholl performed in front of an estimated 80 million people over a 20-year aerobatic career. He also featured in more than 200 movies, documentaries and television commercials.

On 16 September, he was filming a scene that required him to put his plane into a flat spin. Scholl went into the spin, but did not recover and the Pitts fell into the Pacific Ocean off the coast of Southern California. His last words were recorded, "I have a problem. I have a real problem." The precise cause of the crash remains a mystery.

Art Scholl and the plane were never recovered.

INDIAN AIR FORCE TRANSPORT, 1986

Three Antonov An-32 aircraft of the Indian Air Force (launch customer) took off from Muscat, Oman, in a staggered formation on a delivery flight from Kiev in the Ukraine to Jamnagar, India, on 25 March 1986.

Two of them arrived safely. One, from the middle of the formation, disappeared over the Indian Ocean, without a trace. No distress call was heard by the other planes or land stations.

The plane had 3 crew and 4 passengers. The flight path was mostly over water – the Gulf of Hormuz and the Arabian Sea.

There were no mountains on its flight path and generally the route weather was fair.

PAN MALAYSIAN AIR TRANSPORT, 1993

A Pan Malaysian Air Transport Shorts SC-7 Skyvan 3-100 disappeared on 31 January 1993, somewhere over Northern Sumatra.

It was flying from Medan-Polonia to Banda Aceh-Blang Bintang, both within Indonesia.

The Skyvan disappeared over mountains and the last reported position was at 8,500 feet, 67 miles from Medan. It is believed to have crashed into Mt. Kapur in poor weather, including thunderstorms.

Aboard were 14 people; 11 passengers and 3 crew. None have been found.

MERPATI NUSANTARA AIRLINES FLIGHT 6715, 1995

Merpati Nusantara Airlines Flight 6715 disappeared on 10 January 1995 on a flight from Bima Airport to Satartacik Airport, Ruteng, Indonesia, a distance of 123 miles (196 km).

Four crew and 10 passengers were on board. It is believed that the DHC-6 Twin Otter crashed in the Molo Strait in bad weather. Investigators were never able to find the plane or its occupants.

ANATOV AN-72, 1997

A Renan Airlines (Moldova) Anatov An-72 freighter with 5 crew on board disappeared on 22 December 1997 on a flight from Abidjan (Cote d'Ivorie) to Rundu in Namibia.

The plane disappeared without a trace over the South Atlantic. It was speculated by some commentators that the Angolan Air Force may have shot it down.

EGYPTAIR FLIGHT 990 (1999)

A Boeing 767 en route from New York City to Cairo crashed after takeoff on 31 October 1999 killing all 200 people on board. After a two-year investigation, the National Transport Safety Board concluded that the relief first officer in the cockpit had deliberately caused the crash.

The evidence included the trajectory of the plane as well as cockpit voice and data indicating that the captain and first officer had fought for control of the plane in its last moments, as the first officer repeatedly said, "I rely on God." But the Egyptian government disputed that version of events, releasing its own report concluding that the crash was caused by a mechanical failure of the plane's elevator control system.

STEVE FOSSETT, 2008

American adventurer Steve Fossett, 63, set off from Nevada on 3 September 2007 in preparation for solo flight around the world without refuelling.

Fossett was reported missing after the single-engine Bellanca Super Decathlon he was flying over the Great Basin Desert in Nevada failed to return. Despite a month of searches by the Civil Air Patrol (CAP) and others, Fossett could not be found and the search was called off on 2 October 2007. He was declared legally dead on 15 February 2008.

A hiker found Fossett's identification cards in the Sierra Nevada Mountains on 29 September 2008. The crash site was discovered on 1 October 2008, 65 miles south of the Flying-M Ranch where he had taken off.

On 3 November 2008, tests conducted on two bones recovered about one-half mile from the site of the wreckage produced a match to Fossett's DNA.

Vittorio Missoni

VITTORIO MISSONI, 2013

Vittorio Missoni, Italian fashion designer and CEO of the Missoni fashion house founded by his parents in 1953, took off in a 44-year-old Britten-Norman Islander on 4 January 2013 from Los Roques Airport in the Los Roques archipelago, where he had been holidaying, for Caracas, Venezuela.

The plane disappeared and wreckage was not found until almost a year later. The bodies of five people on the plane, including Missoni's wife Maurizia Castiglioni, were recovered but Missoni's body was not found.

A bag belonging to Missoni was found a month later on the island of Bonaire, between Los Roques and the island of Curaçao.

JULY 2014, 462 DEATHS

Three airliners disappeared from the world's skies in July 2014. claiming 462 lives.

Malaysia Airlines Boeing 777 flight MH17 was shot down as it passed over Ukraine with 298 people on Board. TransAsia Airways ATR 72-500, flight GE222, crashed in storms over Taiwan with 48 of the 58 people on board killed and Air Algerie Mc Donnell Douglas MD-83, flight AH5017, crashed in Mali with no survivors from the 116 people on board.

The TransAsia plane crashed while attempting to land at Magong Airport, Taiwan, during a storm and the Air Algerie plane went missing after trying to divert around bad weather en route from Ouagadougou in Burkina Faso to Algiers. The plane's wreckage was found in Mali's Gossi region, not far from the border with Burkina FasoIts.

The TransAsia crash was quickly identified as a result of bad weather but the Air Algerie crash, though attributed to bad weather, also involved suspicion about an attack on the plane in an area where rebellion activity was known.

Adventurer Steve Fossett poses next to his aircraft the Virgin Atlantic Global Flyer

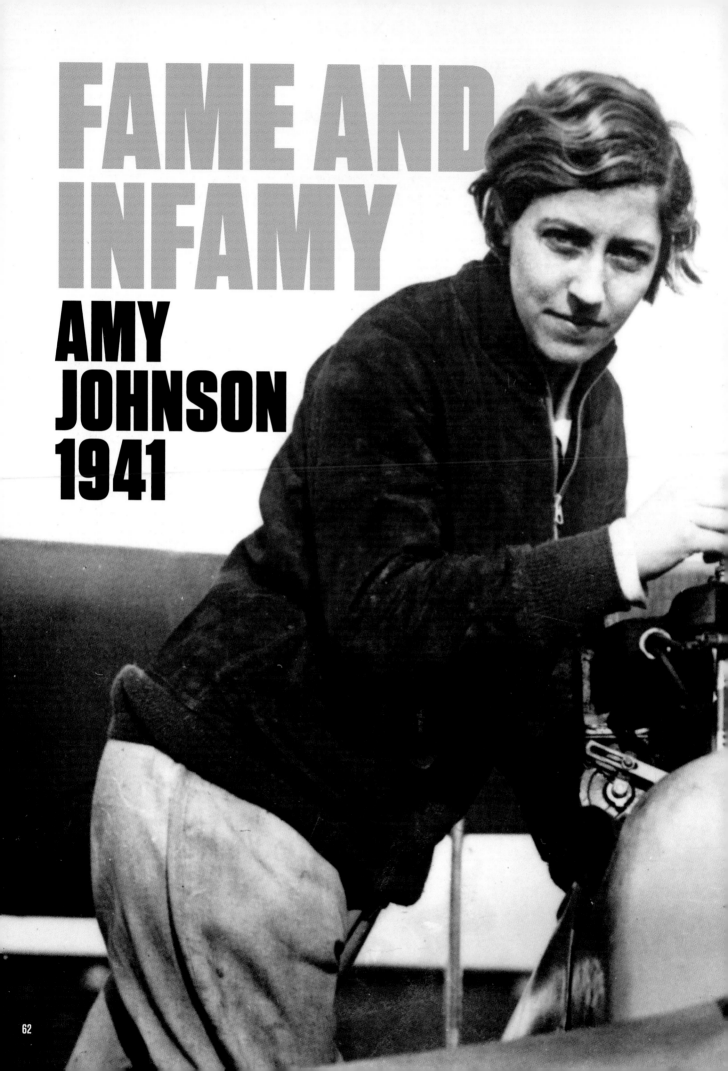

FAME AND INFAMY

AMY JOHNSON 1941

Mystery still surrounds the death of pioneering English flyer Amy Johnson in 1941 because details of her flight remain a government secret

But more than 50 years later it has been claimed she was shot down by gunners from her own country because she did not respond with the correct codes when challenged.

Amy Johnson flew in World War II as a member of the Air Transport Auxiliary and died during a ferry flight on 5 January 1941.

Her first major achievement, after flying solo, was to qualify as the first British-trained woman ground engineer, and first woman in the world to do so.

Early in 1930 she set an objective to fly solo to Australia and beat Bert Hinkler's record of 16 days. She set off from Croydon on 5 May 1930 and landed in Darwin on 24 May, a flight distance of 11,000 miles. She received worldwide recognition as the first woman pilot to fly solo from England to Australia and returned home to the UK to a hero's welcome and was awarded a Commander of the *Most Excellent Order of the British Empire* (CBE) honour.

In 1932 Johnson married Scottish pilot Jim Mollison and in July that year she set a solo record for the flight from London to Cape Town, South Africa, in a Puss Moth named *Desert Cloud*, breaking her new husband's record. Her next flights were as a duo, flying with Mollison. In 1933, she and Mollison flew a de Havilland DH.84 Dragon, named *Seafarer*, nonstop from Pendine Sands, South Wales, to Bridgeport, Connecticut, in the United States, where upon running out of fuel they crash-landed and were injured. After recovering they received a ticker-tape parade down Wall Street.

In May 1936 Johnson made her last record-breaking flight, regaining her Britain to South Africa record in a Percival Gull Six. She was divorced in 1938 and reverted to her maiden name.

At the outbreak of World War II in 1939, Amy Johnson joined the Air Transport Auxiliary, a pool of experienced pilots who were ineligible for RAF service. Her duties consisted of ferrying aircraft from factory airfields to RAF bases.

On 5 January 1941 while flying an Airspeed Oxford from Blackpool to RAF Kidlington near Oxford, Johnson flew off course in bad weather. Reportedly out of fuel, she bailed out as her aircraft crashed into the Thames Estuary.

Lt Cmdr Walter Fletcher, the commander of *Haslemere*, dived into the water to rescue Johnson but he died in the attempt. Johnson's body was never recovered.

Then in 1999, it was reported that Tom Mitchell from Crowborough, Surrey, claimed to have shot down the plane.

He claimed that Johnson failed to give the right identification code, which was changed every day for all British forces so troops on the ground would know they were British. Apparently, she failed to give the code twice and was shot down as an enemy aircraft. Mitchell said: "Sixteen rounds of shells were fired and the plane dived into the Thames Estuary. We all thought it was an enemy plane until the next day when we read the papers and discovered it was Amy. The officers told us never to tell anyone what happened." There has been no official verification of the claim.

TWA FLIGHT 800, 1996

THE CONSPIRACY THEORY: A missile strike from a terrorist or US Navy ship took out TWA Flight 800 and the incident was covered up by the US Government

THE OFFICIAL VERSION: Over-heated gas in the Boeing 747-100's near-empty fuel tank caused the tank to explode

Members of the press inspect the wreckage of TWA Flight 800

The memorial of TWA Flight 800 at Smith Point Park in Shirley, New York

TWA Flight 800 exploded in mid-air off the coast of Long Island, New York on 17 July 1996, just 12 minutes after take-off from John F. Kennedy International Airport on a scheduled passenger flight to Rome, via Paris.

All 230 people on board died, the third highest death toll from an aviation accident in US territory.

The victims' death certificates were not finalised because "manner of death" remained unknown.

During the investigation, the Federal Bureau of Investigation (FBI) took over the case when a criminal act was suspected. Sixteen months later the FBI announced that no evidence had been found of a criminal act and ended its investigation.

Adding to suspicions, witnesses reported seeing something shoot up towards the plane just before the explosion. Unexplained explosive residue was found throughout the wreckage.

The resulting 4-year-long investigation that included the National Transportation Safety Board, TWA, the Airline Pilots Association, the FBI and third party accident investigators, produced a 400-page official report with the finding that the explosion was caused in a fuel tank by a spark from a damaged wire; an electrical short circuit ignited fuel vapours in the jet's centre wing fuel tank.

But the case remains classified "pending inactive", not closed.

Examination of the cockpit voice recorder and flight data recorder data showed a normal departure with the plane in flight mode before both abruptly stopped at 20:31:12.

The captain is recorded as saying at 20:29:15: "Look at that crazy fuel flow indicator there on number four......see that?" A noise from the last few tenths of a second of the CVR was similar to the last noises recorded from other panes that had broken up in mid-air.

That, with the distribution of wreckage and witness reports, all indicated a sudden catastrophic incident, whatever the cause.

Further interest in the conspiracy theories was sparked in 2013 on the 17th anniversary of the incident.

The Epix TV channel broadcast a documentary which alleged the crash investigation was a cover-up. It contained witness interviews, some interviewees objecting to previous publicly released versions of their descriptions of events. It also featured interviews with investigators who had been involved in the original inquest, 6 of whom had filed a petition to reopen the inquiry. Their petition was based on witness accounts, radar evidence indicating a possible missile and claims of evidence tampering.

According to the conspiracy theory, 2 missiles rose from the ocean while another was fired from Long Island's Patchogue Bay.

One of the holes in that premise is that no evidence of missile fragments was found, according to investigators. Also lacking is a reason missiles would be fired at the plane.

Federal officials have said they stand by their conclusion that the fatal explosion was caused by overheated fuel tank vapours, not a bomb or missile.

ITAVIA FLIGHT 870, 1980

After 33 years of inquiries, parliamentary commissions, expert reports and one of the longest judicial investigations in Italian history, many are still not convinced by the official explanation for the loss of Aeorlinee Itavia's McDonnell Douglas DC-9-15

The plane was flying a domestic route from Bologna to Palermo, Italy, and crashed into the Tyrrhenian Sea between Ponza and Ustica on 27 June 1980. All 81 people on board were killed in the incident that became known as the Ustica affair.

The immediate theory was that it was a tragic accident caused by some kind of mechanical or structural failure. Then there were thoughts that it may have been destroyed by a bomb.

The controversial finding by an Italian Senate committee in 1989 was that the plane was shot down by a missile fired from an unidentified aircraft.

Relatives of those on board were not satisfied with the first investigation and five years later the Italian Government launched a new investigation and recovered the cockpit voice recorder. The recording abruptly cuts off as a pilot starts to say "guarda" – look.

Radar readings appeared to show fast-flying aircraft in the vicinity of the commercial flight. It was contended that French fighter planes were chasing Libyan fighters in a NATO operation. The missile theory was firmed up.

A suggestion that terrorists could have planted a bomb was rejected and in 1999 an exhaustive investigation by Judge Rosario Priore, one of Italy's most respected legal figures and an expert on terrorism cases, concluded that the plane had probably been

Il Messaggero
di Roma

Era partito ieri sera da Bologna diretto a Palermo

Dc 9 dell'Itavia con 81 persone s'inabissa in mare presso Ustica

L'ultimo contatto radio con la torre di controllo di Ciampino. Vane finora le ricerche del relitto. Si teme che non ci siano sopravvissuti

caught in a dogfight between NATO jetfighters and Libyan MiGs.

In his 5,488 page report, Mr Priore said he could not say for sure who had caused the deaths of the 81 people on board. However, he said investigations into the downing of the flight had been deliberately obstructed by the Italian military and members of the secret service, probably at the behest of NATO.

Four generals were tried on charges of treason and obstructing investigations. None were convicted.

It was yet another investigation in 1994 that raised more controversy and mystery. A report on that investigation concluded the plane was blown up by a bomb planted in a lavatory. The report was never released.

That investigation was led by British international investigator Frank Taylor who had worked on the downing of the Pan Am flight over Lockerbie, Scotland, by a bomb in 1988.

Examination of additional debris indicated an explosion had occurred near the back of the plane.

The clue was the discovery of debris from a steel wash basin. Taylor tested the result of a bomb blast on another basin and found the resulting debris was consistent with that found from flight 870.

Taylor also concluded that the images of fast moving objects actually showed debris from the explosion, not other aircraft.

Taylor commented: "We discovered quite clearly that somebody had planted a bomb there, but nobody on the legal side, it would appear, believed us and therefore, so far as we are aware, there has been no proper search for who did it, why

they did it, or anything else. As an engineer and an investigator I cannot see why anybody would want to consider anything other than the truth."

In 2008, Rome prosecutors reopened the investigation into the crash after former Italian President Francesco Cossiga (who was Prime Minister when the incident occurred) said that the plane had been shot down by French warplanes. A claim for damages was served on the French President.

In September 2011 the Palermo civil tribunal ordered the Italian government to pay 100 million euros in civil damages to the relatives of the victims for failure to protect the flight and for concealing the truth and destroying evidence.

Finally, on 23 January 2013, Italy's top criminal court ruled that there was "abundantly" clear evidence that the flight was brought down by a stray missile and confirmed the lower court's order that Italian radar systems didn't adequately protect the skies and the Italian Government must compensate the victims' families.

And a final twist: Some of the Italian Air Force officials who might have known about the disaster's background died suddenly between 1980 and 1995: 2 committed suicide; 2 died in car accidents; 2 air force pilots who crossed flight 870's path on 27 June collided mid-air during the 1988 Ramstein Air Show; one, aged 37, suffered a heart attack; and one was murdered.

This provided fertile ground for conspiracy theorists who believed there was a massive cover-up of something quite sinister.

THE PRINCESS AND THE SAINT RAPHAEL, 1927

Princess Anne of Lowenstein-Wertheim-Freudenberg was obsessed with crossing the Atlantic Ocean by air

Lady Anne Saville was 33 when she married Prince Ludwig of Lowenstein-Wertheim-Freudenberg in 1897. Inside a year the Prince had disappeared. He turned up in the Philippines during the Spanish-American War, believed by some to have been an agent for the German government. He was killed at the Battle of Caloocan.

Anne never remarried but refused to give up her husband's title.

The socialite, aviation patron and daughter of 4th Earl of Mexborough, took her first plane flight in 1914 when she chartered an experimental crescent-wing biplane built by Frederick Handley Page and flown by Rowland Ding for a trip to Paris.

> Because of her marriage to a German and her hunt for an aircraft builder, suspicions were raised that she may have been a spy.

Her story was traced by Daily Observer journalist Sean Chase in a 2013 article. According to Chase, the flight to Paris ignited a passion for flying and the Atlantic became her challenge. She set about getting someone to build a plane for the flight. Because of her marriage to a German and her hunt for an aircraft builder, suspicions were raised that she may have been a spy. This led to her being charged with furnishing false particulars after registering under the Aliens Restriction Order.

Investigators alleged the princess intended to buy planes to carry escaped German officers across the North Sea. She was fined for providing the false particulars about her name but acquitted of any charge that she would be disloyal to England.

She remained interested in flying after the war and bought a plane during an air race in 1922. She became friends with Captain Leslie Hamilton, a flying ace nicknamed "The Flying Gypsy," who flew her plane in the 1923 Croydon to Edinburgh Kings Cup race.

Crossing the Atlantic remained on her mind. She enlisted Hamilton and Lt-Col. Frederick Minchin, a former bomber pilot, for a London-to-Ottawa attempt in a Dutch Fokker F VIIA monoplane bought from the Netherlands. It was named Saint Raphael.

The princess shocked all when she said she would go with them to be the first women to fly across the Atlantic. She arrived at RAF base Upavon in Wiltshire on the morning of 31 August 1927 in her Rolls Royce and dressed in purple leather knee-breeches with matching jacket, black silk stockings and high-heeled fur-lined boots.

The plane took off for Ottawa and was spotted a number of times over Ireland, then by the USS Josiah Macy in the Atlantic as it headed into a bank of fog on the way to Newfoundland.

It is recorded that the plane flew into strong headwinds which would have used up more fuel than expected.

Saint Raphael never made it to Newfoundland. No one knows where it ended up but most likely it crashed into the sea. One of the plane's wheels washed up in Iceland a year later.

Anne was presumed dead by a court order made in London on 6 February 1928.

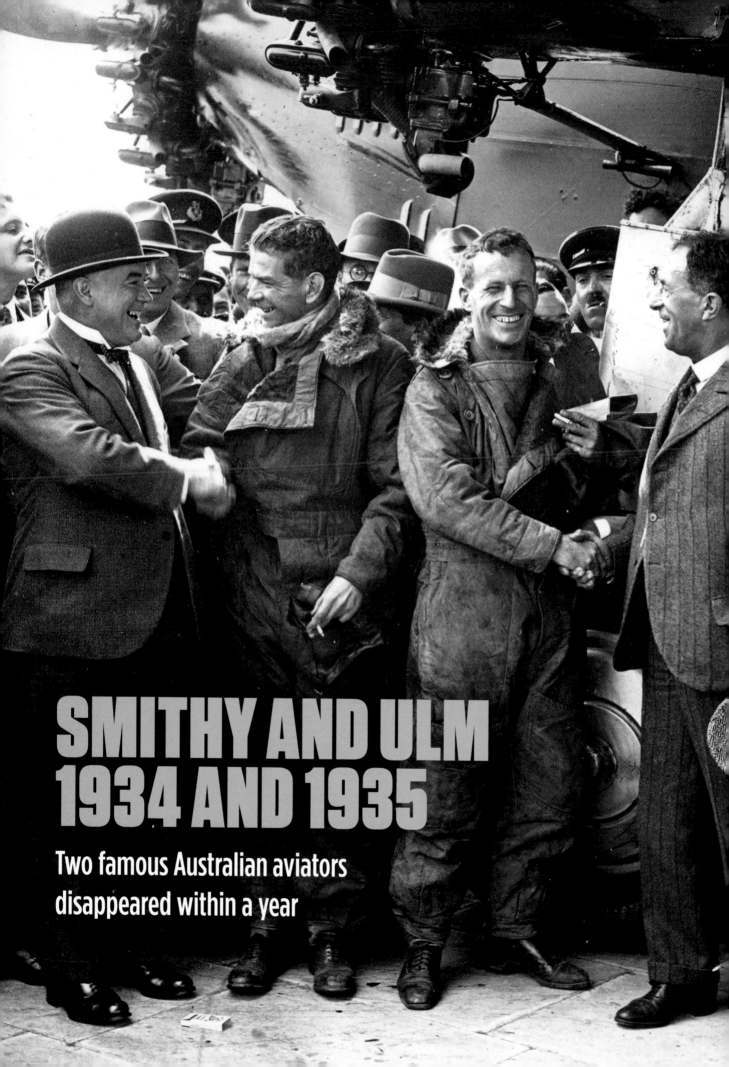

SMITHY AND ULM
1934 AND 1935

Two famous Australian aviators
disappeared within a year

Charles Kingsford Smith and Charles Ulm were a record-setting partnership in aviation feats, including the first crossing of the Pacific.

Kingsford Smith, knighted in 1932 for his pioneering aviation feats, set a number of daring flying records from the 1920s to the 1930s.

In 1928 with Charles Ulm he made the first flight across the Pacific Ocean, flying a 3-engine Fokker named the Southern Cross. They left Oakland, California, with two American crewmen on 31 May. They reached Brisbane via Hawaii and Fiji on 9 June, after 83 hours and 19 minutes flying time. The journey made Ulm and Kingsford Smith popular heroes and both were awarded the Air Force Cross and given honorary commissions in the Royal Australian Air Force.

Also in 1928 they took the Southern Cross on a non-stop flight from Victoria to Perth, the first transcontinental crossing, and made the first trans-Tasman crossing from New South Wales to New Zealand and back.

In 1929 Smithy, as he was affectionately known by then, flew from Australia to London in 12 days 18 hours and in 1930 flew from London via Ireland to New York and San Francisco. Later that year he brought the solo record for London to Australia down to less than 10 days. Three years later he had reduced it to 7 days 4 hours.

His record attempts were to promote the idea that planes had a future as airliners on major routes around the world.

His record attempts were to promote the idea that planes had a future as airliners on major routes around the world.

With J. T. Pethybridge he took off from England on 6 November 1935, aiming to make one more record-breaking flight to Australia. The plane and both fliers were lost. It is assumed they crashed into the sea somewhere off the coast of Burma while flying at night towards Singapore.

Ulm was Kingsford Smith's co-pilot on many adventurous flights and joined him in establishing Australian National Airways in December 1928 to operate unsubsidised passenger, mail and freight services.

Ulm also set records of his own. In 1933 he flew from Australia to England and on the return flight broke the record with a time of 6 days 17 hours and 45 minutes. In 1934 he carried the first airmail between New Zealand and Australia and then returned to New Zealand with the first official airmail to New Zealand.

Hoping to establish a trans-Pacific service between Australia, Canada and the United States, in September 1934 Ulm formed Great Pacific Airways Ltd and bought an Airspeed Envoy, Stella Australis, with long-range fuel tanks. On 3 December 1934, with a crew of 2, Ulm flew from Oakland for Hawaii. Stella Australis failed to arrive. Despite an extensive sea search no trace of the plane or crew was found.

D.B. COOPER 1971

Dan Cooper was the name given by a man when booking a seat and who then hijacked a North West Airlines Flight 305 Boeing 727 aircraft between Portland, Oregon, and Seattle, Washington, on 24 November 1971. The media later mistakenly referred to him as D.B. Cooper.

On board, Cooper opened his brief case and showed what looked like a bomb to a flight attendant.

The plane landed in Seattle where Cooper demanded and was given $US200,000 in cash, 4 parachutes and food for the crew before releasing all the passengers. With 3 pilots and a flight attendant, the plane took off from Seattle and headed south.

It was dark and lightly raining when 45 minutes after takeoff, Cooper sent the flight attendant to the cockpit, put on the parachute, tied the bank bag full of marked $US20 notes to himself, lowered the back stairs and somewhere north of Portland jumped into the night.

A boy digging a fire pit in the sand at a place called Tena Bar in 1980 uncovered 3 bundles of cash just below the surface, with rubber bands still intact. There was a total of $5800 and the Cooper serial numbers matched. A tie identified as the one worn by Cooper also was recovered.

Whether Cooper could have survived the jump was much debated. Significantly, no parachute was found on the ground in the search area.

Then in 2011 an Oregon woman claiming her uncle was the elusive criminal known as DB Cooper says she was told by the FBI that her evidence was enough for them to close the file on the case.

Marla Cooper had told investigators she had a 40-year-old family secret involving an uncle, named Lynn Doyle Cooper.

Marla Cooper said she was eight years old when her uncle whom she called L D Cooper came to her home, badly injured, for Thanksgiving in 1971, the day after hijacking. He had said his injuries were the result of a car crash.

Ms Cooper never saw her uncle again and was told he died in 1999.

She said her uncle had been fixated on a comic book character named "Dan Cooper" the name the hijacker gave to the airline.

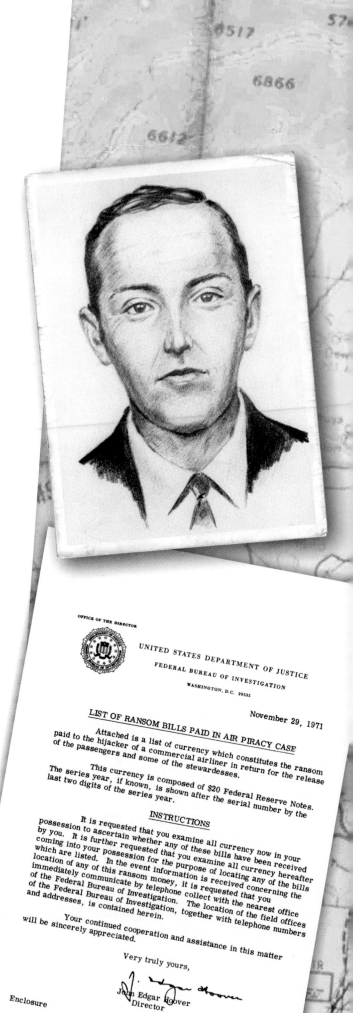

Top: FBI sketch of hijacker D.B. Cooper

Right: A letter from J. Edgar Hoover to the banks regarding the serial numbers on the ransom money

OFFICE OF THE DIRECTOR

UNITED STATES DEPARTMENT OF JUSTICE
FEDERAL BUREAU OF INVESTIGATION
WASHINGTON, D.C. 20535

November 29, 1971

LIST OF RANSOM BILLS PAID IN AIR PIRACY CASE

Attached is a list of currency which constitutes the ransom paid to the hijacker of a commercial airliner in return for the release of the passengers and some of the stewardesses.

This currency is composed of $20 Federal Reserve Notes. The series year, if known, is shown after the serial number by the last two digits of the series year.

INSTRUCTIONS

It is requested that you examine all currency now in your possession to ascertain whether any of these bills have been received by you. It is further requested that you examine all currency hereafter coming into your possession for the purpose of locating any of the bills which are listed. In the event information is received concerning the location of any of this ransom money, it is requested that you immediately communicate by telephone collect with the nearest office of the Federal Bureau of Investigation. The location of the field offices of the Federal Bureau of Investigation, together with telephone numbers and addresses, is contained herein.

Your continued cooperation and assistance in this matter will be sincerely appreciated.

Very truly yours,

John Edgar Hoover
Director

Enclosure

EVIDENCE

From Top to Bottom: A Boeing 727-051 aircraft, FAA number N467US, in March, 1967, on the runway at Cleveland-Hopkins International airport. This is the same aircraft that would later serve as Northwest Orient Airlines Flight 305, hijacked by DB Cooper

Pink nylon parachute canopy from the FBI case file. (Evidence file photo. Credit: Federal Bureau of Investigation)

Green, chest mount reserve container provided to hijacker Dan "D.B." Cooper (Evidence file photo. Credit: Federal Bureau of Investigation)

Recovered ransom monies

A flight test to recreate the jump from a 727 in flight made by DB Cooper. The test was part of the FBI's investigation of the Cooper hijacking, to try and determine the search area for the hijacker

URUGUAYAN AIR FORCE FLIGHT 571, 1972

Roberto Canessa told a newspaper that 40 years on he still remembered vividly having to eat the flesh of friends to survive

Canessa was a passenger on a chartered aircraft that crashed into the Andes mountains between Chile and Argentina on 13 October 1972.

The Uruguayan Air Force twin turboprop Fairchild FH-227D flight was carrying 45 people, including a rugby union team, their friends, family and associates, when it crashed.

More than a quarter of the passengers died and several others fell victim to cold and their injuries.

Of the 27 who were alive a few days after the accident, another 8 were killed by an avalanche that swept over them as they sheltered in the wreckage.

The last 16 survivors were rescued on 23 December 1972, more than 2 months after the crash. The survivors had little food in the freezing conditions at over 11,800 feet up a mountain.

Faced with starvation and hearing news on a transistor radio that the search for them had been abandoned, those who lived fed on the dead passengers who had been preserved in the snow.

Canessa, then a 19-year-old medical student, and another survivor eventually trekked for 10 days to get help. Rescue for the remaining survivors came 72 days later.

The rescue operation took 2 days in difficult weather. All of the survivors were taken to hospitals in Santiago and treated for altitude sickness, dehydration, frostbite, broken bones, scurvy and malnutrition.

Dr Canessa, now a top pediatric cardiologist, and one of 45 passengers that included his Old Christians rugby team, recalled the battle to survive:

"It was repugnant. Through the eyes of our civilised society it was a disgusting decision. My dignity was on the floor having to grab a piece of my dead friend and eat it in order to survive. But then I thought of my mother and wanted to do my best to get back to see her. I swallowed a piece and it was a huge step – after which nothing happened."

My dignity was on the floor having to grab a piece of my dead friend and eat it in order to survive.

ADAM AIR
FLIGHT 574, 2007

The disappearance of Adam Air Flight 574 on 1 January 2007 bore some similarities to that of MH370 7 years later

Flight 574 disappeared from air traffic radar screens almost 2 hours after its 12.55pm departure from the Djuanda Airport in Surabaya, Indonesia, heading for Sam Ratulangi International Airport in Manado, North Sulawesi.

The Adam Air Boeing 737-4Q8 plane was carrying 96 passengers and 6 crew. It was last detected by air traffic controllers in Makassar, South Sulawesi, cruising at 35,000 feet.

No distress calls were made by the captain of the Adam Air flight, Refri Agustian Widodo, or his first officer, Yoga Susanto.

First reports were that the flight changed course twice as

a result of severe crosswind. It was concluded that the plane crashed into the sea.

On 11 January part of a jetliner's tail, food trays and other debris was recovered. On 25 January a US navy ship detected signals coming from the flight recorder.

The flight data recorder and cockpit voice recorder were recovered after a massively expensive search of the seabed 8 months after the crash.

The wreckage and bodies of those aboard were never found.

Indonesian United States National Transportation Safety Board investigators determined the plane crashed because the pilots were distracted by the malfunction of the plane's inertial reference system and had not noticed the autopilot had been disengaged.

The flight also had hit severe weather conditions which may also have been a factor in the pilots missing the autopilot situation.

The Indonesian Bureau of Meteorology and Geophysics reported cloud thickness was "up to 30,000 feet in height and wind speed was at an average of 30 knots in the area."

The plane was said to have encountered crosswinds of more than 70 knots over the Makassar Strait, "where it changed course eastward toward land before losing contact."

A piece of the wreckage of the ill-fated Air Bus A330-200 being lift into a naval ship during search operations

AIR FRANCE FLIGHT 447, 2009

"Damn-it! We're going to crash.
It can't be true!" says a pilot.

"But, what's happening?" another replies.

And with that, Air France Flight 447
from Rio de Janeiro to Paris disappeared
in the early hours of 1 June 2009

A part of the vertical stabilizer of the Airbus A330-200 is lifted from a Brazilian Navy frigate into a truck at Recife's Port

Journalists report the first wreckage pieces and objects of the Air France A330 aircraft

The Airbus A330-200 vanished mid-ocean, beyond radar coverage and in darkness. For 6 hours Air France struggled to come to terms with where its plane with 216 passengers and 12 crew went.

AF447 was 4 hours into its 11-hour overnight journey. By then many passengers would have been asleep. Others would have felt the turbulence the A330 encountered as it flew through a storm.

From the realisation that AF447 had crashed, it took 3 years to resolve the mystery.

The investigation involved costly mid-Atlantic searches covering 10,500 square miles of often uncharted sea bed to depths of 15,000 feet. So remote was the place in equatorial waters between Brazil and Africa it was five days before debris and the first bodies were recovered.

Finally, almost 2 years later, robot submarines located the aircraft's flight recorders.

It was May 2014 before the report by 5 expert investigators pinpointed what they believe went wrong.

They said there was "an inappropriate response from the crew" after the plane's speed sensors malfunctioned; the "predominance of human factors in causing the accident and acting as contributory factors had been clearly established".

The crash could have been avoided if the crew had taken appropriate action, the report said.

The experts also criticised Air France, saying the pilots were not adequately trained to handle unusual situations such as when the speed sensors known as pitots (small, forward-facing ducts that use airflow to measure airspeed) malfunctioned.

Once in the storm, these had apparently frozen over, blanking airspeed indicators and causing the autopilot to disengage. From then on the crew failed to maintain sufficient speed, resulting in a stall which, over almost 4 minutes, sent the plane down. French air crash investigation organisation the Bureau d'Enquêtes et d'Analyses reported that the crew had ignored repeated stall alerts and kept trying to climb, instead of levelling off or descending to pick up speed. Instead of lowering the plane's nose to deal with the stall, as they should have done according to normal procedures, they raised it. The A330 became so slow it simply stopped flying.

But Air France countered that the pilots had "showed unfailing professional attitude, remaining committed to their task to the very end".

The flight recordings showed the plane was responsive up to the point of impact. The investigation confirmed that one of the pilots had pulled the stick back and kept it there for almost the entire emergency. With its nose pointed too far upwards, the Airbus had eventually lost momentum and stalled. Apparently no one else in the cockpit realised this until it was too late.

Despite the latest report, questions remain over the operation of the aircraft, including the positioning and type of controls.

Air France improved training for pilots, concentrating on how to fly a plane manually when there is a stall. Both Air France and Airbus were facing serious charges, with a judicial investigation led by Paris judges ordered.

Pere Lachaise cemetery in Paris shows a funerary stela in tribute to the victims of the Air France Flight 447 Rio-Paris plane crash

---

From the realisation that AF447 had crashed, it took 3 years to resolve the mystery.

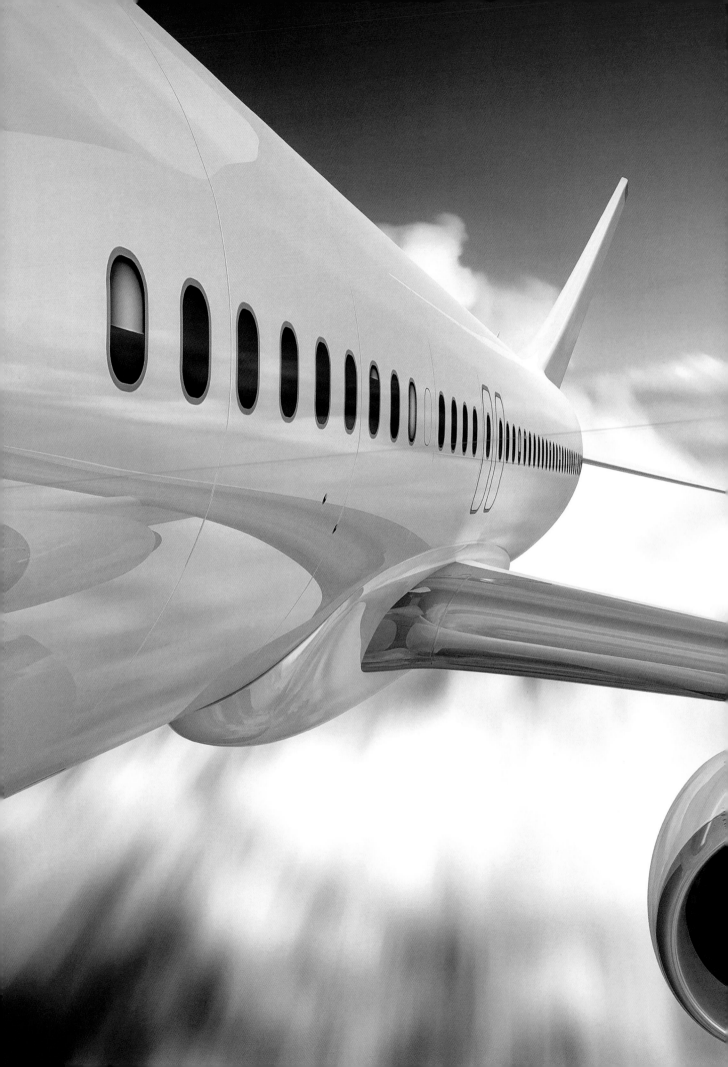

STRANGER THAN FICTION

Aliens, ghosts and the Bermuda Triangle have all figured in mysteries surrounding planes that have disappeared or crashed

THE GHOSTS OF FLIGHT 401

Eastern Air Lines Flight 401, a Lockheed L-1011-1 Tristar jet, crashed into the Florida Everglades on 29 December 1972, claiming 101 lives. There were 75 survivors

Captain Bob Loft and Second Officer Don Repo were preparing for a routine landing as their plane approached Miami airport when a warning light flashed. There was a problem with the landing gear.

The plane quickly lost altitude and crashed. It was the first crash of a wide-body aircraft and, at the time, the second deadliest single-aircraft disaster in the US.

Investigators determined that the flight crew became preoccupied with the indicator light and did not notice the autopilot had been disconnected.

Captain Loft and Second Officer Repo survived the initial impact but both died of their injuries soon after.

The story of Flight 401 should have been the heroic rescue of the survivors. And that was the case until Eastern Airlines began fitting salvaged parts to other planes.

Soon began a stream of ghostly sightings on planes that received parts from Flight 401.

More than 20 reports were made, including by people who had known Loft and Repo. Their ghosts were also identified from photographs by people who had not known them.

Several Eastern crew members reported seeing Repo in the cockpit and the galley of some flights.

They said he was particularly concerned with flight safety, and even fixed a faulty oven circuit once. He had also he pointed out a potential fire hazard and a hydraulic leak.

In one reported sighting a flight engineer was carrying out the routine pre-flight inspection when Repo appeared to him and said, "You don't need to worry about the pre-flight, I've already done it."

It is claimed Captain Loft's ghost was also seen on some flights, sitting in first class or in the crew cabin.

A flight attendant is said to have confronted Loft, asking what he was doing on the plane as she had not seen him board and could not identify him on the passenger manifest. Receiving no reply, she reported it to her flight captain. He walked back with her and recognised Loft, who disappeared immediately in front of a dozen people.

The airline remained sceptical but is understood to have ordered all of the salvaged parts of the ill–fated Flight 401 be removed from the planes that had received them.

Airline sources said once that happened, all sightings stopped.

The ghost stories became a best-seller by author John G. Fuller, *The Ghost of Flight 401*.

*A snapshot from the made for television movie
THE GHOST OF FLIGHT 401 - Pictured: (l-r) Allan
Miller as Les Garrick, Margie Gordon as Didi Wyatt*

A map showing the area know as the Bermuda Triangle

THE WORK OF THE DEVIL

The Bermuda Triangle doesn't show on world maps. The name was coined in 1964 by a magazine which was reporting on the seemingly abnormal disappearances of planes, ships and people in the roughly 500,000 square miles of the Atlantic Ocean bounded by Miami, Bermuda and San Juan, Puerto Rico.

Over years, there has been a seemingly disproportionate number of unexplained disappearances. Some records put the number of planes and ships lost there at 100 and lives lost at more than 1,000.

But the US Coast Guard says the number of incidents is not out of the ordinary.

Yet some people even speculate that it's an area of extra-terrestrial activity or that there is some strange natural cause for the region to be hazardous. Realists say it's just an area where people have had a lot of bad luck.

Perhaps explorer Christopher Columbus is to blame for the mystique surrounding the Triangle. According to his log, on October 8, 1492, Columbus noticed that his compass was behaving strangely. He didn't want to alarm his crew with the information that his compass wouldn't point to magnetic north. Panic is not a good look when you are sailing into the unknown on the oceans blue.

The mystery of the Triangle, also known as the Devil's Triangle, gained traction in 1945 when 5 US Navy Avenger aircraft disappeared there. The cause of the disappearance was originally listed as "pilot error," but family members of the pilot leading the mission wouldn't accept that and convinced the Navy to change it to "causes or reasons unknown."

There were 5 significant aircraft disappearances over the Triangle in 20 years, beginning with the Navy Avengers in 1945.

The others lost without trace and listed in official records were:

- **1948:** January 30, Avro Tudor G-AHNP Star Tiger lost with 6 crew and 25 passengers, flying from Santa Maria Airport in the Azores to Kindley Field, Bermuda.

- **1948:** December 28, Douglas DC-3 NC16002 lost with 3 crew and 36 passengers, flying from San Juan, Puerto Rico, to Miami.

- **1949:** January 17, Avro Tudor G-AGRE Star Ariel lost with 7 crew and 13 passengers, flying from Kindley Field, Bermuda, to Kingston Airport, Jamaica.

- **1965:** December 6, private Cessna lost with pilot and a passenger, flying from Ft. Lauderdale to Grand Bahamas Island.

- **1978:** September 21, Douglas DC-3 of Argosy Airlines with 4 people aboard disappeared off radar over the Caribbean Sea on a flight from Fort Lauderdale International Airport to José Martí International Airport, Havana. The search was called off on 24 September with no trace found.

The US Coast Guard explanation:

First, the "Devil's Triangle" is one of the two places on earth that a magnetic compass does point towards true north. Normally it points toward magnetic north. The difference between the two is known as compass variation. The amount of variation changes by as much as 20 degrees as one circumnavigates the earth. If this compass variation or error is not compensated for, a navigator could find himself far off course and in deep trouble.

LOST AVENGERS

Five US Navy TBM Avenger torpedo bombers comprising Flight 19 began as a routine over-water navigational training mission in 1945. It ended with 6 planes vanishing into thin air

Flight 19, led by Charles Taylor, took off from Fort Lauderdale, Florida at 2.10 pm on 5 December 1945. There were scattered showers in the area but generally the weather was clear and an experienced flight instructor was in the team. But 90 minutes into the exercise the pilots became disoriented and couldn't recognise landmarks below. According to radio transmissions, Taylor's compass malfunctioned and it appeared he was confusing the Florida Keys with the Bahamas. The command tower tried to direct Taylor back to Fort Lauderdale but eventually lost contact and none of the 5 planes was heard from or seen again, believed to have crashed into the rough seas off the Florida peninsula.

A PBM Mariner rescue seaplane with 13 people aboard also went missing that night while searching for Taylor's team. It simply dropped off the radar, leading most to assume it exploded (inexplicably) in mid-air.

Taylor, without giving a reason, had asked to be excused from the day's exercises. The Navy denied his request.

Portrait of legendary Lost Squadron & plane
"Flight 19" that supposedly vanished into
Bermuda Triangle shortly after WWII

Guido Valentich holds a photograph of his son Frederick

VISITED BY ALIENS

What happened to lone pilot Frederick Valentich who disappeared off the Victoria, Australia, coast in 1978, may never be resolved

Valentich had appropriate clearance and experience to undertake the solo night flight to King Island.

A 30 cm long piece of engine cowl from the same model Cessna 182 aircraft he was flying on 21 October washed ashore more than 300 km away at Flinders Island 5 years after he disappeared.

In all likelihood Valentich became disoriented in darkness and crashed into Bass Strait. But doubt remains because of the lack of debris in the area. If he was disoriented it is also possible he crashed many miles off course, even on remote land somewhere.

> ## What deepens the mystery is that Valentich reported by radio that he was being followed by an Unidentified Flying Object.

Eight vessels and an Orion aircraft searched the sea for 4 days but found no trace of the plane.

What deepens the mystery is that Valentich reported by radio that he was being followed by an Unidentified Flying Object. He had at first queried whether there were any other aircraft in the area.

Valentich was part-way through a 7-minute conversation with Melbourne air traffic control about what he was seeing in the night sky near his plane.

"It is not an aircraft it is . . . ," an air-traffic control transcript records him as saying. And a minute later: "What I am doing right now is orbiting and the thing is just orbiting on top of me also it has a green light and sort of metallic, it's all shiny (on) the outside."

And in his final communication: "My intentions are – ah – to go to King Island – ah – Melbourne. That strange aircraft is hovering on top of me again (open microphone for two seconds). It is hovering and (open microphone for one second) it's not an aircraft."

A long metallic clanging sound was heard and the contact ended.

The Royal Australian Air Force said a day later it had received 11 reports from people along the coast claiming to have seen UFOs on Saturday night; the reports were discounted because Valentich's disappearance the previous night was by then common knowledge and likely to have provoked "copycat" sightings.

But according to the Victorian UFO Research Society, based near Melbourne, there had been a UFO wave ongoing for at least 6 weeks before the date of Valentich's disappearance.

An official 315-page official report on the incident left open a finding, even the possibility of UFO involvement.

MYSTERIOUS MESSAGE

A plane and human remains were found 50 years later but what really happened to the Star Dust aircraft, a civilian version of the Lancaster bomber operated by British South American Airways, in 1947 remains a mystery

All investigators have to go on is the last message received from the Star Dust during a snowstorm when it disappeared over the Andes mountains on 2 August 1947. The message ended with "STENDEC".

The Chilean radio operator in Santiago said the reception was clear, but the message was sent rather quickly, so the operator asked for it to be repeated, twice. The message was believed to be the same on all 3 occasions, the final Morse code transmission being "ETA SANTIAGO 17.45 HRS STENDEC" four minutes before it was scheduled to land that day. (Morse code was used until an aircraft was close enough to an airport to make radio contact).

The controller responded that he did not understand the acronym at the end of the message but "STENDEC" was never clarified by the pilot, fuelling conspiracy theories about UFOs.

The wreckage of the aircraft was not found for more than 50 years.

In 1998, a pair of Argentinian rock climbers ascending Mount Tupungato discovered engine wreckage and returned to Santiago to report their alarming find.

An Argentine army expedition in 2000 discovered additional wreckage as well as human remains, including a hand and part of a torso.

The discovery of the wreckage of Star Dust enabled investigators to determine what happened. The plane crashed into the side of the mountain during a storm, possibly causing an avalanche that buried it for all those years.

But the word STENDEC will always be a subject for debate with most popular theories suggesting a miss-keying of the Morse code - STENDEC is an anagram of DESCENT. How it could be done three times though tends to discredit that possibility.

Mount Tupungato where the plane wreckage was found 50 years after it disappeared

Inset: British South American Airways hostess Mary Guthrie about to board the Lancastrian airliner
'Star Dust' at Heathrow Airport, before a test-flight to Buenos Aires

FLYING INTO A STORM

FLIGHT QZ 8501

Indonesia AirAsia Flight QZ8501 flying from Surabaya city to Singapore vanished over the Java Sea on Sunday, 28 December 2014, claiming the lives of 162 people aboard

At first similarities were drawn with the missing Malaysia Airlines Boeing 777 which vanished 9 months earlier. But the disappearance of QZ8501 turned out to be more similar to Air France Flight 447, which crashed in the mid-Atlantic in June 2009 killing 228 people.

The Air France and AirAsia planes, though far apart, were both flying in areas near the equator, where trade winds from the northern and southern hemispheres intersect, causing severe weather from time to time.

According to Indonesia's meteorological agency BMKG, weather was the "triggering factor" in the AirAsia disappearance.

"The most probable weather phenomenon was icing which can cause engine damage due to a

Wreckage from AirAsia flight QZ8501 is lifted into the Crest Onyx ship at sea

cooling process," BMKG said.

An initial 14-page report referred to infra-red satellite pictures that showed the plane was passing through cloud top temperatures of minus 80 to minus 85 degrees Celsius.

Flight QZ8501 took off from Surabaya at 5.20 am local time and was scheduled to land at Changi Airport at 8.30 am Singapore time for the flight of almost 2 hours.

Contact with Jakarta air traffic control was lost at 6:17 am when the plane was almost halfway to Singapore. There was no distress call.

On board were 155 Indonesians (including the pilot, Captain Iriyanto), 3 South Koreans, and one person each from Singapore, Malaysia and Britain. The co-pilot was French.

Captain Iriyanto, 53, had 20,537 flying hours, 6,100 of them with AirAsia on the Airbus A320. The first officer, Remi Emmanuel Plesel, 46, had 2,275 flying hours.

The plane was flying at 32,000 ft (9,753 metres) and the pilot had asked to climb to 38,000 ft (11,577m) to avoid a significant storm front just before contact was lost 42 minutes after take-off. The request was refused at the time because of heavy plane traffic in the area. When air traffic controllers granted permission to fly at 34,000 ft (10,361 m) a few minutes later there was no response.

Three days later debris was located off the coast of Kalimantan. It was another day before the debris was positively identified and just over a week before any bodies were recovered, some of the passengers still strapped in their seats.

Two weeks after the plane vanished large pieces of the plane were identified and the first item, the plane's tail, was brought to the surface. At that time searchers also said they had also pinpointed where the flight recorders were – they had become separated from their housing in the tail.

The area where the flight disappeared is notorious for bad weather. At the time the region was being pummelled by heavy storms with extensive flooding in Malaysia and the Philippines.

Search operations were hampered by bad weather and fast currents.

The Airbus operated by AirAsia's Indonesian affiliate had accumulated 23,000 flight hours in 13,600 flights. Its last scheduled maintenance was on November 16. Airbus delivered the plane (registration PK AXC) to AirAsia in 2008.

AirAsia and its affiliates had never lost a plane previously before and had a good safety record.

Indonesia AirAsia operated 30 A320s. Across all of its subsidiaries and affiliates AirAsia operated 170 A320s.

When air traffic controllers granted permission to fly at 34,000 ft (10,361 m) a few minutes later there was no response.

In late January 2015, Indonesian authorities announced they were suspending the search for more bodies after finding no more in the wrecked fuselage of the plane on the sea floor.

Bad weather had constantly hampered recovery efforts.

An interim official report on the crash was not made public, however the Transport Minister said that after the crew had been refused permission to fly higher to avoid a storm, local radar had detected the plane travelling upwards much faster than normal. It had mostly likely stalled, he said.

One report that came to light from the investigation was the belief that the co-pilot had control of QZ8501 at the time of last contact.

AirAsia and its affiliates had never lost a plane previously before and had a good safety record.

SHOT DOWN - 857 KILLED IN 3 HITS

The shooting down of 2 civilian planes, KAL007 and Iran Air 655, in a decade of animosity during the 1980s Cold War claimed 559 lives

Then in 2014 a civilian airliner was shot down over Ukraine, claiming another 298 innocent victims of conflict between the Ukraine government and a separatist movement loyal to Russia.

Explanations were given but suspicion and mystery remained.

Truth appears to have been a casualty as well as the 857 lives taken so violently in these 3 acts of aggression.

According to Wikipedia, around 1400 lives were claimed by live fire on airliners from 1950 to 2014.

Some were shot down after straying into prohibited airspace, others were shot down by ground forces engaged in rebellions. Some were claimed to have been shot down by accident.

MH FLIGHT 17

As if Malaysia Airlines didn't have enough to deal with amid the search for Flight MH730, the shooting down four months later, on 17 July, of flight MH17 on its way from Amsterdam to Kuala Lumpur was catastrophic

All 298 lives on board were lost as a missile took out the plane 33,000 feet above Ukraine where separatists were engaged in conflict with the government of Ukraine. The wreckage rained down near the village of Grabovo, in Ukraine's Donetsk region.

The separatists were quickly blamed by the Ukrainian Government which said rebels had recently stolen a Buk surface-to-air missile system from a Ukraine depot. There were also accusations that the launchers and missiles had come from Russia. Whatever their origin, the system was capable of hitting targets of altitudes up to 15 miles.

A transcript of an intercepted telephone call , if genuine, allegedly made by a separatist leader to a Russian intelligence commander left little doubt that the separatists shot down MH17, probably mistaking it for a Ukraine military plane.

All 298 lives on board were lost as a missile took out the plane 33,000 feet above Ukraine

But Russia was similarly quick to lay blame on the Ukraine government, saying the Kiev leadership was responsible for the ongoing conflict with separatists and because the plane was shot down in Ukraine territory, Ukraine was responsible. Rebel leaders denied they had anything to do with the shooting down and they and the Russian leadership tried to implicate the Ukraine military.

The investigation was always going to prove difficult with the plane coming down in a region controlled by separatists. It was plagued by controversy from the start with reports recovery teams were initially prevented access, unsupervised removal of bodies and wreckage including flight recorders, and a failure to secure the crash site.

Whatever the truth of the downing of MH17, tension around the world increased dramatically as a result.

And whatever the outcome of investigations and repercussions, the world was not likely to forget the atrocity any time soon.

KAL FLIGHT 007, 1982

The shooting down of a Boeing 747 Jumbo passenger plane by a Soviet fighter plane in 1982 could have easily sparked war between the West and the Soviet Union

The attack on Korean Airlines Flight KAL007 on 1 September took the lives of all 269 people on board the flight from New York to Seoul via Anchorage.

It was shot down by a Soviet Su-15 interceptor near Moneron Island, west of Sakhalin Island, in the East Sea.

The Soviet Union at first denied knowledge of the incident, but later admitted the shoot-down, claiming the aircraft was on a spy mission and was in Soviet airspace when it was attacked.

The Soviets said it was a deliberate provocation by the United States to test the Soviet Union's military preparedness, or even to provoke a war. The US accused the Soviet Union of obstructing search and rescue operations. The Soviet military suppressed evidence sought by the International Civil Aviation Organization investigation, particularly by not handing over the flight data recorders, which were eventually released 8 years later after the collapse of the Soviet Union.

Study of the flight recorders eventually led investigators to conclude that the KAL pilots had made a mistake on their operational settings but believed they were still on course. Their mistake meant they strayed into Soviet airspace, twice.

Meanwhile, the Soviets had been tracking a US reconnaissance mission operating in a similar area. The straying passenger jet raised alarm and fighters were scrambled.

Col. Gennadi Osipovitch, pilot of the fighter that downed Flight 007, was to say many years afterwards he first thought

Japanese TV simulation of KAL Flight 007 being shot down by Russian jet for spying

the Jumbo was a civilian flight because of its flashing lights but said military planes could be disguised as civilian planes. He said the flight crew should have seen the warning shots he fired before he was ordered to take it down with missiles.

"I wondered what kind of plane it was, but I had no time to think," Osipovitch recalled in an interview with CNN. "I had a job to do. I started to signal to (the pilot) in international code. I informed him that he had violated our airspace. He did not respond."

One of those on board was Lawrence McDonald, a House of Representatives member from Georgia in the US.

The whereabouts of the bodies of Flight 007 remains a mystery.

Once investigators examined the flight recorders they established that missile fragments "hit the back of the plane, destroying 3 of its 4 hydraulic systems, severing some cables and punching holes in the aircraft's walls".

The damaged plane flew on for 12 minutes as it spiralled downwards and crashed into the sea.

Some remains and personal effects washed ashore in Wakkanai, Japan, in 1983.

It is generally accepted that pilot error in engaging the autopilot caused the plane to stray off course. Suggestions the plane was part of a US spying mission have virtually been ruled out although suspicion remains about its flight path and the actions of the Soviets.

*n of how the USS
anian Airbus over
US demonstration*

Five years after the downing of Flight 007, the US brought down an Iran Air Airbus A300, Flight 655 from Tehran to Dubai

The crew of the US Navy's USS Vincennes Navy mistakenly identified the plane as an attacking fighter jet and fired on it, killing all 290 passengers (including 66 children) and crew.

When Iraq invaded Iran in 1980, the United States supported Iraqi leader Saddam Hussein against the two countries' mutual Iranian enemy. The war dragged on for eight years, with thousands of lives lost.

On July 3, 1988, the USS Vincennes was swapping fire with small Iranian ships in the Persian Gulf. The US Navy presence there continues to this day, protecting trading routes.

The US version of events was that the Airbus was mistaken for a fighter plane and did not correctly identify itself so Vincennes fired at it.

The attack took place in Iranian airspace, over Iran's territorial waters in the Persian Gulf, and on the flight's usual path.

The event generated a great deal of controversy and criticism of the United States. Some analysts blamed US military commanders and the captain of Vincennes for reckless and aggressive behaviour in a tense and dangerous environment.

The International Course of Justice records that in 1996, the United States and Iran reached "an agreement in full and final settlement of all disputes, differences, claims, counterclaims".

As part of the settlement, the United States agreed to pay $US 61.8 million, an average of $213,103.45 per passenger, in compensation to the families of the Iranian victims.

Subsequent investigations for the National Geographic television program Air Crash Investigation confirmed the airliner was transmitting an identification "friend or foe" code for a civilian aircraft, but Captain William C. Rogers III of the Vincennes insisted he believed the code alone did not mean the aircraft was non-hostile. Captain Rogers described the attack as a self-defense measure to save his ship and the lives of the crew in the belief that they were going to be attacked by a fighter plane.

Though making ex-gratia payments, the US denied having any responsibility or liability for what happened.

From Top to Bottom: Relatives of victims of the Iranian Airbus stand under a painting depicting the scene

A row of shrouded caskets holding the victims of an Iranian Airbus with a crowd of mourners behind them at Parliament

Thousands of people mourn in Tehran, during the funeral service for those who died on the Iran Air passenger jet

View of USS Vincennes, the cruiser that mistakenly shot down an Iranian passenger airline killing all aboard

TERROR IN THE SKIES
PAN AM FLIGHT 103

Civilian airliners have also been the target for terror attacks, claiming hundreds of lives

Pan Am Flight 103, a transatlantic flight from Frankfurt to Detroit via London and New York City, was destroyed by a terrorist bomb on 21 December 1988, killing all 243 passengers and 16 crew on board. The wreckage rained down on the Scottish township of Lockerbie.

A former Libyan intelligence officer, Abdelbaset al-Megrahi, was convicted of bombing the flight. Colonel Muammar Gaddafi admitted responsibility for the Lockerbie bombing in 2003 and agreed to pay 1.7 billion pounds compensation to the families of the dead. But in 2014 a former Iranian intelligence officer, Abolghassem Mesbahi, who defected to Germany, claimed Flight 103 was brought down in retaliation for the US Navy strike on an Iranian commercial airliner six months earlier.

Some of the wreckage of Pan Am Flight 103 after it crashed onto the town of Lockerbie in Scotland

Inset: Mug shots of alleged Libyan intelligence officials Abdel Basset Ali al-Megrahi and Lamen Khalifa Fhimah, suspected of fabricating the bomb which blew up Pan Am flight 103

Aircraft debris and destroyed houses in the village of Lockerbie

Evidence of what is believed to be fragments of the bomb which blew up Pan Am Flight 103

PP8932

PI/995

Cms 1 2 3 4 5

9/11

The terror attack on the US on 11 September 2001 has been well documented

Four passenger airliners were hijacked by 19 al-Qaeda terrorists to be crashed into major buildings.

American Airlines Flight 11 and United Airlines Flight 175 were crashed into the North and South towers of the World Trade Center in New York City. American Airlines Flight 77 was crashed into the Pentagon (the headquarters of the United States Department of Defense) and United Airlines Flight 93 was targeted at Washington DC but crashed into a field near Shanksville, Pennsylvania, after passengers tried to overcome the hijackers.

The attacks killed almost 3,000 people on the planes and in buildings and, according to the Institute for the Analysis of Global Security, caused at least $10 billion of property and infrastructure damage.

THE WAY AHEAD

The Malaysia Airlines Flight 370 case prompted extensive debate about steps to be taken to prevent airliners disappearing from the world's skies

After the events of September 2001 when terrorists in the United States hijacked airlines and crashed them, significant steps were taken to improve security. Reinforced doors were installed at the entry to the flight decks of passenger planes. A number of countries appointed armed air marshals to join selected flights. Intensive screening procedures were set up at airports and restrictions introduced on carry-on items.

Now there have been calls for additional security doors to be fitted to further restrict access to the cockpits of passenger planes.

Safety experts have advocated the introduction of remote flying technology so ground-based personnel could take control of flying the plane away from those on board. There have also been suggestions that unmanned drone technology could be further developed for use on larger freight and even passenger planes.

Another proposal is that pilots and flight crew be refused the ability to turn off transponders and tracking devices once a plane is in the air.

The International Air Transport Association (IATA) has started work with the United Nations International Civil Aviation Organisation on systems that allow better tracking of planes.

Better co-operation between civilian and military radar operations has been urged amid suggestions various countries don't want others to see what they are actually capable of.

But generally the aviation world seemed resigned to the fact that airliners could be brought down no matter what procedures were in place, as evidenced by the Malaysia Airlines Flight MH17 incident.